T0267191

# A HOME IN WOODS HOLE

## LIFE AND HISTORY ON EEL POND

Elizabeth Heslop Sheehy

THE
History
PRESS

Published by The History Press
Charleston, SC
www.historypress.com

*Front cover*: A view of Eel Pond from School Street in the 1920s, with Walter Nickerson's house in the background. *Woods Hole Historical Museum.*

First published 2024

Manufactured in the United States

ISBN 9781467156769

Library of Congress Control Number: 2024935278

*Notice*: The information in this book is true and complete to the best of our knowledge. It is offered without guarantee on the part of the author or The History Press. The author and The History Press disclaim all liability in connection with the use of this book.

*To my parents, without whom nothing else was possible*

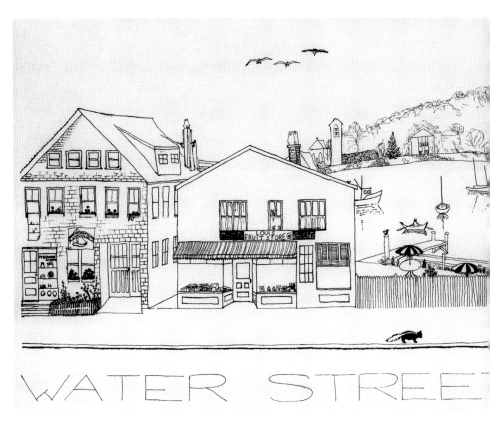

*Water Street, Woods Hole*, pen-and-ink drawing. *S. Robyn Kanwisher*.

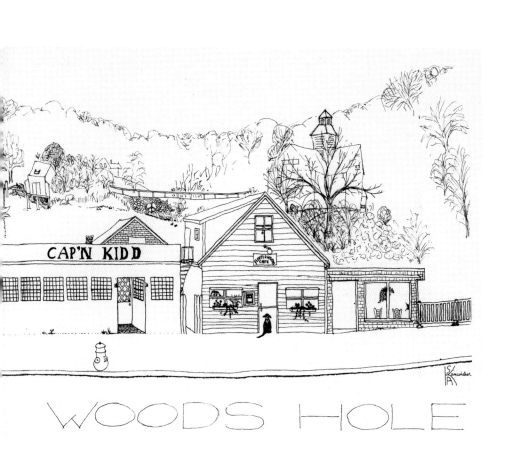

WOODS HOLE

# CONTENTS

# CONTENTS

# FOREWORD

Like all great mystery stories, Elizabeth Sheehy's *A Home in Woods Hole: Life and History on Eel Pond* begins with a question. The "whodunit" in this case: Who built my newly purchased old house? Hunting for an answer, Elizabeth found the path far from straightforward. The first misleading clue concerned the age of the house, advertised in real estate listings as being constructed in 1890. Not so, as it turns out. Determined to solve the mystery, Elizabeth takes us on a fascinating journey, digging through the archives at the Woods Hole Historical Museum, examining old town records, consulting with colorful locals and encountering the occasional serendipitous breakthrough that all historians hope for.

As she illuminates the lives of previous residents of her beloved house on Millfield Street, she tells the larger story of Woods Hole, from its early whaling days to its present-day incarnation as home to world-renowned scientific institutions. This tiny village that once produced noxious guano-based fertilizer for farms across America went on to produce Nobel Prize winners and today hosts thousands of visitors from around the globe. Through dogged investigative work, Elizabeth discovered the answer to her central question and much more. But a few mysteries remain unsolved, in particular the fate of fourteen-year-old Dorothy Nickerson—a member of the family who built the house—who appeared in the 1940 U.S. Census and then disappeared.

Both the author's successes and failures at fact-finding highlight the vital importance of preserving the artifacts of our past. Without historical documentation, we lack the tools to understand and interpret events shaping our own lives today. As the late historian David McCullough wrote: "History is who we are and why we are the way we are."

We at the Woods Hole Historical Museum are proud to play a role, albeit a small one, in collecting and safeguarding items that help bring local history to life. Our handwritten letters, deeds, ship's logs, photographs, articles of clothing, maps, oral histories and even small boats allow us to envision the past more fully and to understand it more accurately.

It was one of these artifacts—a 1910 map of Woods Hole—that provided Elizabeth with one of her first significant clues about the age of the house on Millfield Street. On the map, the site of the house is not on Eel Pond but *in* Eel Pond. She subsequently learned that the Nickerson family built their house on landfill.

It has been immensely gratifying for the museum to assist the author in her fact-finding mission and in the preparation of this intriguing book highlighting the history of Woods Hole. We hope that it serves as a reminder to anyone cleaning out a relative's home, attending an auction or scoping out antiques stores that what looks like junk might be a key piece of evidence in someone's search of the past. In fact, one of our museum's most treasured items, an 1881 diary written by sixteen-year-old Ruth Anna Hatch, was salvaged from a dump in the nearby town of Bourne.

As you will learn in reading this book, Woods Hole is a place of discovery. From the author's vantage point on Eel Pond—a name that belies its beautiful setting—you can see the laboratories of the Woods Hole Oceanographic Institution, the classrooms of the Children's School of Science and the specimen collecting boats of the Marine Biological Laboratory. Still more lies just beyond, including our museum.

In *A Home in Woods Hole: Life and History on Eel Pond*, Elizabeth Sheehy takes us on her own voyage of discovery. It's a wonderful ride and a wonderful read. Enjoy!

Sara Piccini
Executive Director
Woods Hole Historical Museum

# Preface

## *The Lure of Old Houses*

This story begins in 2018, when my husband and I took a huge leap of faith and purchased a century-old house on Cape Cod. There were a million reasons—in the form of a million needed repairs—*not* to buy the house, yet we could not resist the opportunity to own this distinctive property. Whatever draws us to old houses defies logic. Old houses demand our attention—and our money—capturing our hearts and haunting our souls.

For some it is the architecture: sweeping staircases, graceful rooms, authentic decorative details and historic integrity. Others long to test their craftsmanship, rescuing derelict buildings from the brink of ruin. And then there are the mystery seekers, looking for secret rooms or valuable items in the attic and wondering about the people who lived there. I fall into the latter category, focused on learning about the design, purpose and occupants of old houses. Beyond their beauty are the stories of the people who lived there, tales of success and failure, great actions and painful memories. Investigating the history of our house on Eel Pond, I was reminded that every house has unique stories, and every family has interesting people in its ranks. Bringing to light these extraordinary lives, shaped by the cultural climate of the day, is the best kind of treasure hunt and one that never really ends.

My research morphed beyond the house and its occupants. Their stories were intricately tied to the rhythm of the village itself. I discovered that the people of Woods Hole possessed exceptional resilience and resourcefulness, moving away from one dying industry and repurposing their skills to fit the next opportunity. From farming to whaling, shipbuilding to factory work, kitting up sailors for long sea voyages one century and day-trippers for island jaunts the next, life evolved economically while also seeming to stand still.

Studying the two families at the heart of this book—the Nickersons and the Nugents—revealed a bounty of remarkable characters. I knew better than to romanticize the hardships suffered by the farmers or the seamen, by mothers losing babies in Illinois and Falmouth, businesses going bust, spouses dying unexpectedly. These setbacks were an all-too-familiar part of life in the nineteenth and early twentieth centuries. I could not help but admire, however, the resolve with which the struggling figures carried on in the face of adversity. Giving up was not an option, but they did not go it alone. Family and faith kept them moving forward, and with few exceptions, their hometowns welcomed them back again and again.

Most of the questions about our old house were answered satisfactorily, illuminated by extensive research and serendipitous encounters. I confirmed details about the building's construction and gained some understanding of the economics of converting it to multifamily living. Along the way, this exploration deepened my appreciation for the enormous evolution of Woods Hole through the centuries, from a sleepy farming hamlet in the 1700s to the world-class scientific powerhouse of the twenty-first century.

Researching the people central to the house was not nearly as simple. Documentation was limited to census data and newspaper articles. Without private letters or photos, I couldn't flesh out the personalities of the individuals, although occasionally I got a glimpse of them through rare first-person recollections. Mary Ramsbottom, niece of the original owner's daughter-in-law, gave me her firsthand assessment of the lady of the house. She assured me that while the owner's sister Gertrude Nugent was lovely and warm, her sister Helena "was not."[1]

But to this day, there is one mystery that remains: Who is Dorothy? In the course of researching each branch of the Nickerson/Nugent family tree, I came across Dorothy Nickerson, purportedly the fourteen-year-old daughter of the childless Joseph and Frances Nickerson. She appeared on the 1940 Census and never again. There is a story behind her inclusion on the official document, but despite exhaustive effort, I have yet to resolve it. Perhaps that will be a pleasant by-product of my writings. Someone out there may hold the key to this mystery. WHO IS DOROTHY?

# Acknowledgements

This book could not have been written without the efforts of historic preservation visionaries, including those who prioritized the digitization of local newspaper archives and those who protected older buildings from demolition. I am especially grateful to the *Falmouth Enterprise* for 125 years of exceptional writing, former editor Bill Hough's encouraging words and for consistently reporting on the daily activities that forge a community. The team at the Woods Hole Historical Museum provided guidance and unfettered access to maps, photographs and the stories of Woods Hole's people, keeping alive the spirit that has sustained the village since 1603. Many thanks to Susan Witzell, Deborah Griffin Scanlon, Colleen Hurter and Sara Piccini for their support and to Rob Blomberg for setting us on the trail of our home's mysterious beginnings.

Over the five years of researching and writing this book, innumerable people helped with the project: archivists and architects, Woods Hole natives and historians, writers and editors and many a patient friend. While I can't mention everyone by name, I must mention a few: Miriam Kleiman and Thora Colot, whose encouragement and knowledge of NARA were invaluable; Susan Laird for her writing guidance; Paul Marrone for bringing the story of the Wachusetts Dam to life; Terry Ingano for his insights on the life of Father John O'Keefe; Bill Roslansky, who has explored/repaired nearly every corner of our house on Eel Pond; Mary and Sara Ramsbottom, who provided the only tangible personal links to the house's original owners; Falmouth Historical Society's Meg

Costello, who offered great insights into my project; Debra Lawless and Brian Nickerson, who shared insight into Nickerson family history; Sarah Flynn and Celia Slater for their gentle critiques and helpful suggestions; Chris Cedrone and his construction team for bringing the house into the twenty-first century; and Erica Capobianco, the realtor who guided me away from—and then toward—our glorious house.

I am indebted to The History Press, not only for having faith in my story and publishing this book, but also for the previously published books that served as outstanding research tools for this project. Mike Kinsella, who green-lighted the book, Abigail Fleming and her gentle edits, Maddison Potter's marketing efforts and the wonderful (though anonymous to me) team that designed a cover even more beautiful than I had imagined. Well done!

Many thanks to the friends and family who listened to stories from decades past, offering suggestions for further research and crisper writing. In particular, thank you to my siblings, Jacqueline, Dorothy (and her maps and charts prowess) and John; Alexandra and Hanson; Natalie; Robin; Dana; Gayle; Dick Jason; Tilly; my Hecht's Girls; everyone at WHHA who endured the Woods Hole storytelling; and my fabulous college crew, Karen, Kim, Jenny, Marceline and Jen. And finally, my family deserves a medal for support, starting with my mother-in-law, Helen, our super superintendent, who made this venture work; Emma (my tech consultant); TR (steadfastly supportive); and Jackson (who visited dozens of cemeteries with me on various road trips); Salem (the cat) who kept me calm; and most especially Tom, my partner through the madness of it all. Throughout the house purchase, renovation and book writing, he kept the faith that it would all work out, and it did.

# INTRODUCTION

## *Fitting in to Village Life*

N ew Englanders are known for their steely reserve, their distinctive regional accents, their grit. With few exceptions, they live and breathe Red Sox in the summer and Patriots in the fall, with Celtics and Bruins filling the rest of the seasons. They will accept outsiders, so long as those outsiders agree that Dunkin' beats Starbucks, New England clam chowder beats that red stuff from Manhattan and nothing beats watching the Winter Classic hockey game at Fenway Park in January. I know this as a Californian who married a boy from Massachusetts.

Every New England town and village has its own unique personality. Cities like Boston and Worcester have long been melting pots for immigrants from Ireland and Poland and more recently from Vietnam and Ukraine. Drink a few Sam Adams, and one can claim to be Bostonian. The smaller towns require a bit more time and effort to fit in, even more on seasonal Cape Cod. Each of the fifteen towns on the Cape differ, some more artsy, others offering shopping or long stretches of beach. Woods Hole is one of eight villages that makes up the town of Falmouth, and it evokes a quirkiness—a mix of historic buildings and state-of-the-art scientific study—all its own. And as one finds throughout New England, there is a palpable hierarchy within the village population.

At the top of the pyramid are the old families. Even today there are residents who grew up in the village, as did their parents and grandparents. Giffords, Swifts and Geggatts live in the area many generations after their forebears arrived in the nineteenth century, or earlier. Some who grew up in the village left for a time but have returned to year-round living. In many ways, these founding families are the soul of Woods Hole and retain the stories, along with photos and keepsakes, that provide continuity to village history.

One might debate who comes next in the hierarchy, but long-term summer homeowners have the advantage of permanence over students and service workers who generally are year-round renters. Every June, these summer residents return to a well-established routine of sailing, swimming and sunsets. Students and service workers who live in the village throughout the year, however, are better tuned to the daily rhythm of restaurants and cultural events around town.

As in any summer town, tourists rank at the bottom of the ladder, appreciated for supporting the local restaurants and shops, though equally bemoaned for the congestion they bring. Since Woods Hole is the terminus of the Steamship Authority ferry to Martha's Vineyard, these travelers mostly limit their time to an hour or two waiting for their transport. Some visit the Woods Hole Aquarium or the museum, while others make a mad dash for the boat ramp with only minutes to spare.

My husband and I are balanced in a precarious spot on this ladder. We are newcomers, outsiders. Tom's mother, Helen, lives there year-round, along with our full-time tenants. Technically, Tom and I are homeowners in Woods Hole, paying taxes and hiring local professionals to deal with our many issues, but we recognize that, living and working in Virginia, we are still visitors when we slip into Woods Hole to work on the house or enjoy a few days' respite.

I first came to Woods Hole in my early twenties, a "day tripper" headed to Martha's Vineyard for a day of biking and beaches. My husband's connections to the village stretch much farther back, visiting family who lived in nearby Cataumet. As a child, Tom learned to fish off the jetty near the U.S. Fisheries buildings. In the summer, his uncle took him fishing off the Elizabeth Islands in his Boston Whaler, and they would sell their catch upon returning to the town dock off Albatross Street. Though an avid fisherman and native Cape Codder, Uncle Dick does *not* eat seafood; his interest lies in sport and financial gain.

My father-in-law, Tom-the-elder, fell in love with Woods Hole as a high school student in the 1950s, working in the Marine Biological Laboratory (MBL) kitchen during the summer. He played pickup softball games on the ballfield off Bell Tower Lane, behind St. Joseph's Church,

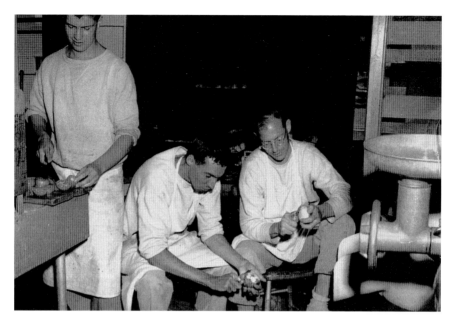

Tom Sheehy Sr. (*left*) working in the MBL kitchen in 1951. *MBL Archives.*

and he frequented the Leeside Tavern, a watering hole near the ferries preferred by working-class locals. Occasionally, he would hang out at the Captain Kidd, domain of college kids working in the WHOI labs. He witnessed firsthand the critical work of the United States Coast Guard Station at Woods Hole, located on Little Harbor, which has protected the coastline since 1857. It was no surprise, then, that he spent a few years in the Coast Guard after attending Boston University. His love of Woods Hole ran deep and was lifelong. It is both fitting and bittersweet that his death six months before we bought the house was instrumental to our ultimate purchase.

On the night before his funeral in January 2018, the immediate Sheehy family drove from Natick down to Woods Hole for dinner in honor of the family patriarch in his favorite spot. As we settled into a table in the back room of the Captain Kidd, woodstove aglow and locals enjoying the post-Christmas calm, we looked across Eel Pond at the house that had occupied my dreams (more on that later). Helen, despite her grief, soaked up the warmth and commented on the comforting atmosphere of the familiar restaurant. Six months later, the house was ours and Helen was preparing to move in.

Someday Tom and I will attend the Church of the Messiah regularly, participate in the civic activities of the library and museum and enjoy lectures at the academic institutions. For now, we remain content during our sporadic sojourns to meet our neighbors, immerse ourselves in the village atmosphere and dig into the history and architecture of our old house. We may not be old-timers yet, but at least we are no longer day trippers.

# Book I
# The House

---◆---

*He bought a crooked cat, which caught a crooked mouse,*
*And they all lived together in a little crooked house.*
*—Anonymous*

# 1
## How It All Started

In 2018, we bought a house on Eel Pond in Woods Hole, Massachusetts, a tiny village on Cape Cod. The rest, as they say, is history.

Though we nurtured Cape Cod fantasies for years, our odyssey really began with the MV20, a twenty-mile road race on Martha's Vineyard that traverses the surprisingly hilly island in February, because who wouldn't want to run twenty miles on Martha's Vineyard in *February*?[2] The diehard runners travel from across Massachusetts—and even Virginia, like my husband, Tom—to test their grit against the New England elements. In February, rest assured, there *will* be elements. In fine Massachusetts fashion, the race culminates with a bowl of steaming hot clam chowder in a middle school gym. I've never seen Tom look so joyful eating soup.

While Tom ran the grueling race (its motto: No Weenies), my son and I drove the course, stopping occasionally to cheer him on or check out the empty beaches. In July, this route would be packed with cars and bikes and beachgoers. But in February, the winter wind whipped at us from every direction, keeping our beach explorations brief. Admiring the lovely, lonely homes that would welcome summer people in a few months, I found myself daydreaming about these gray beauties and the people lucky enough to own them. Browsing the internet (just looking, thanks!), I fell in love with a house my family neither needed nor could afford. And just like that, my obsession began.

The house was enormous. And old. It had been on the market for several years. Built in 1890, it had clearly seen better days. But it was also

Millfield house entry hall. The wallpaper was selected several decades ago by the Roslansky children, and an artist friend hand-painted the interior water pipes to match. *Sheehy Collection.*

on the water, not in the way houses are sometimes described as being "on the water." This 4,500-square-foot behemoth was built 30 feet from the water, with a century-old seawall and stunning views across Eel Pond to Woods Hole. But the feature that captured my attention wasn't the classic Cape Cod gray-shingled elegance or the amazing view. I fell in love with the entry hall.

Twenty years earlier, we fell in love with our home in Virginia in much the same way. After a long day of house-hunting in the Washington, D.C. area, we toured a home that had none of the features so carefully described to the realtor: brick construction, center hall Colonial, in a very specific neighborhood and please, please, no split levels. We found ourselves stopping in front of a white clapboard farmhouse with green shutters, in an unfamiliar school district, and of course, it was a split level. The realtor's note was "has the right feel." Stepping into the glass-enclosed mudroom, it was clear that this was the perfect house for us. That was also the day I realized that the best realtors truly earn their commission.

Back to that cold, windy day in February, I was enchanted by photos of the house in Woods Hole. The entry hall looked like something out of *Fawlty Towers*, the John Cleese comedy, complete with tiny mail cubbies and over-the-top wallpaper featuring ferns and a great deal of yellow. In the center of the room, a sweeping staircase led up to a Palladian window. A closer look might have revealed the shabbiness that comes from years of heavy use. Yet the space conveyed an undeniable warmth, light spilling across a wide window seat that begged the viewer to curl up and read a book. The photos conveyed elegance and history and potential. It was a bed-and-breakfast fantasy!

The next six months were spent investigating the property from a few scant photos, attempting to create floorplans and imagining the flow of the spaces. In August, while Tom ran his first Falmouth Road Race,[3] a bucket list item, it was time to contact the realtor and start asking questions. She was unavailable to show the house that week, yet even over the phone she did not attempt a hard sell, having gone down this path before with many, many Cape Cod real estate dreamers. Built in 1890, it had been subdivided into five separate apartments and rented year-round to Woods Hole locals. It was a maintenance nightmare, with five kitchens, six bathrooms, six boilers and other endless items that required upkeep and/or replacement. Not an easy sell, for sure! Still, the potential was evident, and in October I finally flew up to Boston, drove down to the Cape and went inside. I would either come to my senses, or not.

Joining the house tour were three excellent advisors: my mother-in-law, Helen, who is supremely practical; her brother-in-law, Dick, a Cape Cod native and expert on all things related to old houses; and a builder friend of his who could offer an unemotional assessment. Helen pointed out all the cracks, rust and other niceties, while Dick and his friend wandered the building in silence. At the end of the tour, Dick stood outside at the edge of the seawall, arms outstretched as he took in the beauty of Eel Pond, with Woods Hole framing the scene. "This," he began, with great enthusiasm, "this is magnificent. This," he repeated, taking in the evening light over the still water, "is spectacular. This is unbeatable!"

Turning slowly to face the house, he raised his arms again and, with great flourish, announced, "THIS," nodding to the house "…is a lot of work!"

# 2

# BUILT IN 1890...OR NOT

Against all logic, in June 2018 we bought the house, with its five kitchens, six bathrooms, leaking roof, missing shingles and multiple tenants. After we were handed the keys, the scope of the project took shape. Plumbing, electrical, plasterwork, all needed attention. That the building would need some work was no surprise, considering it was built in 1890, and we were prepared for that. The surprise came when we discovered that the house was not built in 1890 at all.

Initially, there was no reason to question the house's age. The MLS listing was straightforward—Year built: 1890. The basic layout of the structure appeared little altered, a center hall Colonial, with symmetrical rooms featuring five-panel interior doors coming off the main staircase landings. The banister, with its beautiful curled newel and simple, square balusters, reflected popular Colonial Revival details and dominated the heart of the building. The wooden mantels of the five fireplaces appeared to be original, carved with sturdy fluted columns, squared corners. There was an evident addition on the south side of the house, which threw off the building's symmetry, that contained a back staircase leading up to the third floor, providing egress for the upstairs rooms, possibly for servants. It all made sense, at least on the surface, that the house was built in 1890 with an addition put on some years later.

The first clue that all was not as it seemed came during a visit to the village museum. The Woods Hole Historical Museum (WHHM) is a delightful and vital resource for the village. With Woods Hole's off-season population of 850 (growing to 3,500 in the summer months), the museum punches above its weight. Located just up the road from the Steamship Authority ferry terminal, which launches daily transport to and from Martha's Vineyard, the WHHM is a gateway into Woods Hole history and daily life. Billing itself as "a lively small museum with changing exhibits and diverse programs appealing to people with wide interests," the museum campus includes the Small Boat Museum next door and is also affiliated with the Woods Hole Library. Founded in 1973, its mission is keeping alive the living history of Woods Hole.

No visit to Woods Hole is complete without a stop at the museum. The exhibits are entertaining and informative and work for all ages. Objects, photographs and narrative are mined from the rich collections in the archives, offering a unique village-centered perspective. The dramatic exhibit on the Hurricane of 1938, a storm that hit the village with terrifying strength, would give any new homeowner pause, but it helped us feel connected to our new community.

Joining the museum's weekly walking tour of the village, led by guide Rob Blomberg, a Woods Hole resident and part time guide at Fenway Park, we were in for a shock. The tour followed the map in Susan Fletcher Witzell's *The Walking Guide to Woods Hole Houses*, a compilation of building descriptions around the village. Rounding the corner of School and Millfield Streets, Rob mentioned that our house, identified as the Millfield Apartments, was built in the 1930s and suffered significant damage in the Hurricane of 1938.[4] That could not be correct! It made no sense that the house was built in the 1930s. The architectural details of the house—along with the narrative we had already begun weaving in our imaginations about the past residents— did not fit the notion of a 1930s house. And yet, there it was in black and white, in a booklet published by the Woods Hole Historical Museum, lending the information credibility.

I am by nature a puzzle person, consuming jigsaws, crosswords and murder mysteries with gusto. I like to seek out problems and find the right solution. So, while we laughed it off in the moment, the ambiguity about our house's origins did not sit well. I determined to answer when the house was built. What better place to begin the hunt than with the museum archivist herself.

Susan Witzell clarified that much of the information in her booklet came from homeowners and anecdotal information passed down through the years, so while she could confirm the house existed in the 1930s, there was no record of when it was constructed. However, she was fairly certain it had

View across Eel Pond from the southwest corner in 1895. The Millfield house should appear in the far left, proving that the house was not yet built. *Woods Hole Historical Museum (WHHM).*

*not* been built in 1890 as advertised, based on several photographs of Eel Pond from 1895 in which our house was nowhere to be found.

*Caveat emptor*, buyer beware, but of course that phrase is too often ignored. The real estate listing described the house as a five-unit Victorian, built in 1890. With 20/20 hindsight it was clear that the Victorian designation relied on the suggested 1890 build date rather than the building's architectural characteristics. The house did not feature the off-center front door, ornate trim or bay windows typical of Victorian houses.[5] In fact, it is a Colonial Revival house, featuring a hipped roof, accentuated front door frame and symmetrical grouped double-hung windows. With its shingled exterior, however, these disparities were easy to overlook and 1890 did not seem an unreasonable construction date, making it Victorian by age, if not style. However, the 1895 photographs confirmed that the house, in its current state, was not built in 1890. What could explain why it was misidentified?

Recordkeeping is the bedrock of a researcher's life. One takes for granted that records signify facts, data that can support narratives, solve mysteries and answer important questions. Recordkeeping for some vital statistics has been maintained religiously, religiously in the literal sense, as recording births, deaths and marriages in centuries past was undertaken by church offices to keep track of these important rites within the church body. Eventually, these responsibilities shifted to municipal offices, bringing greater consistency to the recordkeeping process while seamlessly ensuring continuity of vital data. In the modern age, we take for granted accurate recordkeeping, not just for civil activities but also in the real estate world. Tax records, building permits, specifics of a building's age are publicly available and play into decisions when purchasing a property.

But it wasn't always this way, and the modern armchair historian needs to be alert for questionable data. In Woods Hole, a building boom took place as industry evolved, starting in the 1870s and continuing through the turn of the twentieth century. Then, as now, the need for housing for a growing workforce in Falmouth was acute, and building construction took off. Many structures were completed with little fanfare and even less documentation. It became accepted practice by the Town of Falmouth that a building of unspecified age—but approximate to the turn of the century—would be listed as "built in 1890." There were a lot of houses built that year, at least on paper.

Within days of making such a significant purchase, it was clear that we knew very little about the house on Eel Pond. The confusion surrounding the house's history kicked my curiosity into overdrive, and I was determined to get to the bottom of it. But first, we had to deal with the issues in need of immediate attention.

## 3

# THE HUNT BEGINS

The months that followed the house purchase were filled with roofers, carpenters, plumbers and painters, repairing the external cladding and renovating one unit for Helen (who had pointed out the rust, cracks and myriad issues during the inspection process). Throughout the renovation marathon, the issue of the house's age continued to nag.

There were three main questions that needed answers:

*1. When was the house built, and by whom?*
*2. Who else has owned or lived in the house prior to 2018?*
*3. When was it divided into apartments, and why?*

One approach to verify the age and history of the house would be to treat it like a science fair project. Starting with the assumption that the house was built between 1895 and the 1930s, the scientific method calls for in-depth research to confirm data points, narrowing down the timeline and then building out the narrative as additional facts emerge.

The great thing with the science fair model is that failure can be an acceptable and exciting part of the process. When an experiment hits a dead end, scientific methods are employed to validate or eliminate certain variables, leading to more accurate conclusions. This was the approach adopted when tracking down information about the house, finding data to narrow the timeline, and indeed it took many an unexpected turn. After a time, going down rabbit holes was no longer a bother, offering up useful but unforeseen information, though it required discipline to stay on track.

So, where to begin?

The mystery surrounding the origins of the house on Eel Pond unfolded at the Woods Hole Historical Museum, so that seemed a good place to start the search for answers. Since the 1970s, local families have donated valuable documents and objects that flesh out the daily life of Woods Hole over the past two hundred years. Among the letters and postcards, photographs, receipts and other remnants of life, there are plenty of maps, and I hoped these maps would establish the timeline of our house's construction.

One of the most beautiful maps in the Woods Hole collection is the 1910 map from the *Atlas of Barnstable County*.[6] Maps such as this did not identify properties by house number, but rather, the properties were labeled with the owner's name. The inconsistent use of house numbers made the task of confirming the construction status of our house at 22 Millfield all the more difficult. A significant portion of Woods Hole remained undeveloped at that time, including the south side of Millfield Street, where only the eastern portion closest to School Street had been developed by 1910. The remaining land edging the northwest shore of Eel Pond was quite narrow and undeveloped, part of the Joseph Story Fay estate.

Focusing on this single stretch of land, it was easy to head down the wrong path. The 1910 map indicated that J. Phillips owned the westernmost house on the south side of Millfield Street. Further research through newspaper archives from 1914 revealed that J. Phillips owned property at 24 Millfield, where he hoped to establish a business. Conflating these two facts, it wasn't unreasonable to assume that the house adjacent to Phillips on this map, the one owned by J. Connors, was 22 Millfield. However, that did not make sense from a spatial perspective.

From a strictly visual standpoint, the westernmost lot appeared to be 18 Millfield, which 1914 data indicated was owned by J. Rohan. If that were indeed the case, then our house was not yet built in 1910. And of even greater concern, the 1910 map made it hard to understand how *any* house could have been built west of that spot, as the strip of land narrowed significantly.

Reconciling the conflicting evidence was a challenge, but not impossible. Further digging confirmed that the developed property at 18 Millfield was indeed owned in 1910 by John Phillips, who would sell the property

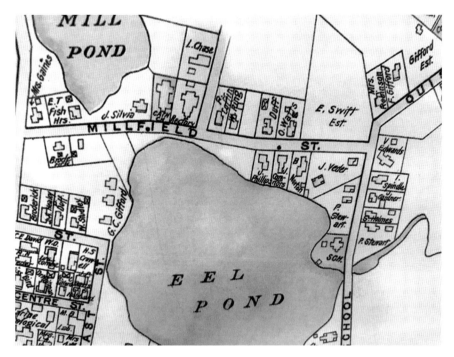

Sanborn Fire Map detail of Millfield Street, 1910, illustrating that the property where the Millfield house now sits was not yet created with fill. *Library of Congress.*

to Jeremiah Rohan in 1911. Apparently, Phillips wanted a larger lot, as he intended to build a service garage on his property.[7] The property he purchased became 24 Millfield as shown on the 1914 records.

Uncovering the Phillips-Rohan land swap, along with comparing the 1910 map to current property lines, made it clear that 22 Millfield was not yet built in 1910. It did not resolve, however, how *any* houses could have been built on the narrow property on the edge of Eel Pond. As there are two rather substantial homes in that area today, something was off. It would take a bit of luck and further investigation to solve that mystery. For the time being, it was satisfying to reduce the potential time frame for the house's construction by twenty years, putting it sometime between 1910 and the 1930s.

As for John Phillips, his vision for building a garage ran into a roadblock in 1915 when he applied for a license for his intended business, facing stiff opposition from his neighbors. At the license hearing, "The residents on Millfield street and owners of adjacent property were present and vigorous protest was made against granting of a garage license on the ground that it would depreciate the value of the property on Millfield street, increase insurance rates, might become a nuisance and would be a continual source of danger."[8]

Among the neighbors protesting was Father Kennedy, pastor of St. Joseph's Church, which sits across the street at 33 Millfield Street. Millfield had been used primarily as an access road, and the small cottages along it were inhabited mostly by immigrant factory workers. But by the dawn of the twentieth century, Millfield Street had begun to come into its own, with larger homes owned by established Woods Hole families, including Swift, Veeder and Sylvia. Father Kennedy wanted Millfield to thrive as a residential street. The concerned residents prevailed, and John Phillips's request was denied. Instead, he invested in a commercial garage north of the Steamboat Wharf, and he was left with a large property with plenty of Eel Pond frontage.

The next stop in the property search was a deep dive into legal documents from the twenty-first century. On a plot plan of the property, prepared for the house closing, is a notation for "existing seawall license #3867." Some creative googling linked this detail to the petitioner's name, Walter E. Nickerson of Falmouth, who submitted plans and an application request to build a seawall on his property on Millfield Street in 1914. Uncovering the legal notice from the *Falmouth Enterprise* added some much-needed clarity.

> *Notice is hereby given that Walter E. Nickerson of Woods Hole has made application to this board for license to build a sea wall and fill solid in Eel Pond in Woods Hole in the town of Falmouth, as per plans filed with said application; and Tuesday, the 28th day of April, 1914, at 11 o'clock, A.M., and this office, have been assigned as the time and place for hearing all parties interested therein.*[9]

Bingo!

No house yet, but this provided several critical answers in one search. The map from 1910 looked funny because some of the land on which the house was built did not yet exist. The seawall had to be completed to "create" the lot (fill solid) before the house could be constructed, which did not happen until at least 1914, thus lopping another four years off the house's potential construction date range. License #3867 allowing the seawall construction was approved on June 30, 1914.[10]

And someone named Walter E. Nickerson held the permit to build that wall. Walter E. Nickerson was the best clue to date.

In the midst of these discoveries, a rather amazing coincidence came to light—the sort of unbelievable connection that gives one pause—and further heightened the urgency to solve the mystery of the Eel Pond house. After my mother-in-law moved into her new apartment in late August, her friend Mary Ramsbottom[11] asked over the phone from whom the house was purchased. The Roslansky name clearly meant nothing to Mary, but on further inquiry, she revealed that she had connections to a house on Eel Pond, owned by her uncle (her mother's brother-in-law). She remembered visiting shortly after the Hurricane of 1938. She was only six at the time and was not allowed to wander around, but she vividly recalled the large living room with a grand piano in the corner. Her sister was fourteen and, as such, was permitted in the back garden by the seawall. Her sister recalled watching a boy in a small boat dredging things out of Eel Pond blown in by the hurricane, including a ten-dollar bill, a small fortune in those days.

*Lo and behold, her uncle's last name was Nickerson!*

According to Mary, Walter E. Nickerson was her uncle Joseph's father, and she was told that he was a sea captain. Her sister still had a set of teacups he supposedly brought back from one of his voyages to China.[12] She heard stories about crew members from Captain Nickerson's ship sleeping in the rooms on the third floor. Mary's aunt Frances Bryne married Joseph Nickerson, who was Walter's only son, but they had no children. It was her understanding that the house was donated to Woods Hole Oceanographic Institution (WHOI) in the 1940s when her uncle was ill. Many of these details turned out to be incorrect, but each contained snippets of the true story.

Though she had limited access to its rooms, it was clear from Mary's description of the house and confirmation of the Nickerson name that Helen was living in the home previously owned by her friend's uncle and that her apartment, now divided into two rooms, once was the spacious living room of the grand home. The information about Walter's maritime career meshed with comments made by various construction crews during the recent renovation, as several commented that this was clearly a captain's house. It was unclear what specific details led to this conclusion, but it did feel as though the pieces were falling into place.

Armed and reenergized with these additional clues, while slightly spooked by the serendipity of it all, I returned to the hunt to find out more about the house's history.

# 4

# EXCAVATING THE FACTS

Whether one is a writer or a police detective, investigative projects require clarity of the five Ws: Who, What, Where, When and Why. This particular investigation was giving up its secrets slowly. Only the actual subject matter—WHAT: the house on Eel Pond—was self-evident, insofar as it was a house. WHO: Walter E. Nickerson—he seemed the likely owner, but the information remained circumstantial. Even the location was murky, as initially the house appeared to be built on nonexistent land, leading to a likely conclusion—WHERE: the house was built on reclaimed land on the edge of Eel Pond. As far as WHEN the house was built, it was narrowed down to sometime between 1914 and 1938, and it was hard to fathom WHY such a large house was built in this particular location. That is all there was to go on, and it was not much.

A detective might have witnesses or experts in the field to answer questions, but all the subjects of this mystery were long dead. Fortunately, one could draw on local property records and a lively local newspaper to provide invaluable keys to this puzzle. To that end, it was time to dig through Barnstable County document archives of the early twentieth century in search of property deeds.

Do not be fooled by the quiet, calm, perhaps even dusty reputation of archives. Just as a picture speaks a thousand words, a legal document—which may contain a thousand words—can add clarity and truth unparalleled by other, more subjective accounts. I envisioned weeks spent in a dark basement room, somewhere on the outskirts of Hyannis, surrounded by reams of files, hoping to find a needle in a haystack of deeds and financial documents. I totally underestimated Yankee ingenuity.

Barnstable County, founded in 1685, has over three centuries of property ownership history, covering all of Cape Cod, in its Registry of Deeds. Property records are public records, and the property records in the Barnstable archives begin in 1742. The Land Court records begin in 1898. Lucky for me, nearly all of the records are available online and are therefore accessible on a laptop from anywhere. With great anticipation, I clicked the large, inviting button labeled "Free Public Search" and started to dig.[13]

Having access to the Barnstable County property records online was a game changer. Barnstable's records are digitized, meaning they are searchable, so typing in "Walter E. Nickerson" produced every public record filed with the county in his name. Discovering the first document was a rush, and each document led to another. Not every document made sense on first glance, but after unearthing them all, several pieces of the puzzle fell into place.

The search for "Walter E. Nickerson" produced four deeds, one license and one mortgage.

The license document was the same License #3867 found on the map of the property, approved on June 30, 1914, to build a seawall and "fill solid" in Eel Pond per the plans submitted. But what were all the other documents?

The first deed listed, recorded on April 15, 1902, corresponded to a house on Middle Street in Woods Hole sold by Vesta and Clarence Gifford to Walter E. Nickerson on December 11, 1901.

The next deed, recorded on July 2, 1913, was for the sale of Lot A (Millfield Street) from the Fay Estate to Walter E. Nickerson on June 19, 1913. This sale took place a year before Walter submitted his application for the seawall license.

The third deed, recorded on November 1, 1916, is especially fascinating. It records the transfer of the property on Millfield, inclusive of the land conveyed by the government with License #3867, to Helena C. Nickerson on October 14, 1916, giving husband and wife joint tenancy. This is a curious action on Walter's part but was made somewhat clearer by the next document recorded in both Helena and Walter's name, which was a mortgage.

The mortgage, recorded on August 31, 1918, was actually signed on October 14, 1916, the same day as the deed transfer. The mortgage agreement was between Helena C. Nickerson of Falmouth, Massachusetts and John J. O'Keefe of Dalton, Massachusetts, with Walter E. Nickerson as a co-signer. It was witnessed by one G.R. Nugent (whose role would be clarified later) in Berkshire County in western Massachusetts and extended $10,000 to the Nickersons, with repayment to O'Keefe of $11,000. No other terms for repayment were specified.

Who was John J. O'Keefe, and why was he extending a mortgage to the Nickersons? Answering questions surrounding the mortgage was yet another mystery that would have to wait, but understanding its purpose was mission critical. In today's dollars, that $10,000 would be worth nearly $300,000, and in 1916, it would build a pretty substantial house on Eel Pond. As a result, the project's hypothesis was tweaked: the house on Millfield Street was built around 1916. But the hypothesis still required proof.

Fast-forward three (yes, three) years. Renovating the top-floor apartment, putting on a new roof, painting the trim, managing a full-time job and family, all these things stymied efforts to track down additional data points on the building of the house. Investigation required time, uninterrupted time, and fewer distractions to lay out facts, see the patterns and connect the dots. Joyce Carol Oates famously stated that the "only thing that's bad for writing is being interrupted. You have to have time to write. And while that seems obvious, you're probably living a life with a lot of interruptions." Indeed I was, and it was time to focus.


SINCE THE LATE NINETEENTH century and still today, the communities of Woods Hole and greater Falmouth get their news from the local newspaper, the *Falmouth Enterprise*.[14] The importance of keeping a community engaged through the dissemination of local news and shared interests cannot be overstated. It binds neighbors together at a micro level, whether the topic is local flora and fauna, high school sports or even more contentious issues such as development or parking regulations.

When the newspaper was established in 1886, Americans' appetite for news was surging. The invention of the linotype in 1884 revolutionized newspaper publishing, making it possible to offer daily papers across the country. The printing equipment was expensive, however, and relied heavily on paid advertising to cover costs. Publishers struggled to avoid offending advertisers, which sometimes resulted in watered-down editorials and skewed feature articles. When the Hough family took over the paper in 1929, the husband-and-wife team were both trained professionals, having attended the Pulitzer School for Journalism at Columbia University, and they committed to eliminate such conflicts of interest.

For a local paper, the reporting and writing are outstanding, and its small staff covers a wide range of issues, including local politics, schools, cultural events and sports. With deep roots in the community, the paper is a good source for early twentieth-century information, though one envisions a laborious process of scouring articles to uncover pertinent facts. And once again, I underestimated the resources available in Falmouth.

Thanks to a grant from the Community Preservation Committee under the Massachusetts Community Preservation Act of 2013,[15] editions of the *Falmouth Enterprise* from 1896 through 1962 were recently digitized and are available online. The search function is impressively sophisticated, allowing for searches with varying degrees of specificity. One can hunt for any articles that reference Millfield Street, for example, or limit searches to specific word sequences or names. Searches can further be defined by date. While it took several weeks of nonstop study, coming up with key words that might get results, every day produced another piece of the puzzle.

The searches constantly evolved, based on what was uncovered, changing directions as discoveries indicated. In the process, a great deal was learned about the comings and goings of the Nickerson clan in Woods Hole during the first half of the twentieth century. The local paper documented shopping trips to New Bedford and the arrival of houseguests from out of town, as well as births, deaths and the inevitable storms.

One day, after plugging in "Millfield Franklin Gifford" (while looking for information about Franklin Gifford's boathouse, built on the lot he owned next to Walter Nickerson's), this popped up:

> Franklin L. Gifford has the contract to paint the interior of Walter Nickerson's new house on Millfield street.[16]

Franklin L. Gifford (1854–1936) is a household name in Woods Hole, a local housepainter who shifted his talents to oil painting after his retirement in 1930. His paintings of Woods Hole's past grace the walls of the Woods Hole Library, and he was once described as the Grandma Moses of Woods Hole.[17] He also owned the sliver of property (Lot B) adjacent to Walter Nickerson's (Lot A) and apparently earned the contract to paint the Nickerson House in 1917. Like the connection between Helen and Mary, niece of Joseph Nickerson, this find is another example of serendipity guiding the research into the Eel Pond house mystery. That was not the information being sought, but it was essential to solving the puzzle. Eureka!

In short order, it all fell into place:

*John M. Howe, contractor and builder, has the contract to build a house for Walter Nickerson on Millfield street.*[18]

*Sumner C. Burgess, electrical contractor, has been awarded the contract for wiring Walter Nickerson's new house on Millfield street.*[19]

*William C. Davis of the Falmouth Furniture Store has the contract to furnish Walter Nickerson's new home on Millfield street.*[20]

And finally, the icing on the cake:

*Mrs. Walter Nickerson and sister, Miss Nugent of Dalton, are stopping for a few days at Mrs. Nora Duff's. Mrs. Nickerson came here to inspect her new house on Millfield street.*[21]

Five years after first spotting the house online, I could confidently conclude that construction of the Nickerson House on Millfield Street in Woods, Hole, Massachusetts, began in 1916 and was completed in 1917.

Who, What, Where and When (and question no. 1) were now answered!

THE ANSWER TO QUESTION no. 2—Who else owned the house on Millfield prior to 2018?—proved to be much easier to resolve. With online access to the Barnstable County Registry of Deeds, finding the previous owners was pretty straightforward. Having identified Walter E. Nickerson as the first owner in 1913, it was easy to follow the thread transferring deeds from one owner to the next. Tracing the property records verified that there have been five owners (or groups of owners) since the property was first purchased from the Fay Estate.

**1. 1913–1945**: Walter Nickerson purchased the land on Eel Pond in 1913 from Henry H. Fay and Sarah B. Fay, the heirs of Joseph Story Fay, who at one time was the largest landowner in Woods Hole. In 1910, this property was undefined land within the Fay estate. By June 1913, it had been subdivided into three lots, plus two tiny spots of land, designated D and E. Walter purchased "Lot A" with forty feet of frontage on Eel Pond, adjacent to "Lot B," with only twenty feet of frontage. In 1914, Walter received a license to build a seawall, creating the land on which the house was constructed. Walter was not a traditional sea captain, as Mary Ramsbottom had been told, but was in fact a mail carrier, contracted by the government to carry the mail by boat to and from the Tarpaulin Post Office on Naushon Island, just off the coast of Woods Hole. He was also a lobsterman. The house stayed in the Nickerson family for another twenty years after Walter's death in 1925.

**2. 1945–1951**: Edward A. Norman purchased the property from the Nickersons in 1945. Norman, son of one of the founders of Sears & Roebuck, was a wealthy New York financier, yet he was beloved in Woods Hole for his stewardship of the Woods Hole Yacht Club in the 1930s and elected commodore in 1940. He also was committed to the Woods Hole Cooperative, on whose board he served for many years. Edward and his family lived in a large "cottage" on Penzance Point, and he purchased the more modest Nickerson House on Eel Pond for unknown reasons. He had just returned to the United States after serving in the U.S. Navy, rising to the rank of lieutenant commander. In the years that followed, his marriage fell apart. He kept his home on Penzance Point but sold the house on Millfield at the time of his divorce.

**3. 1951–1966**: Sidney and Josephine Lawrence bought the house from Edward Norman in 1951. The Lawrence family had deep roots in Falmouth, and Sidney was known for a wide array of occupations, from pig farming to road construction. He served as senior warden at the Church of the Messiah and also on the Falmouth Planning Board. By the time he purchased the property, Sidney was seventy years old, and it must have been a lot to keep up with. After making a few changes to the house, he rented the rooms primarily to members of the scientific community. His estate sold the house following his death in 1965.

**4. 1966–2018**: John and Priscilla Roslansky both earned doctorates, he in zoology from University of California, Berkley, and she in microbiology from University of Rochester, before moving to Woods Hole in 1963. They purchased several buildings in the village, including the house on Millfield. The family owned the property for over fifty years, renting the apartments out to students and scientists.

**5. 2018–Present**: Tom and I bought the house in 2018 and spent the next few years uncovering its history.

EACH OF THE PREVIOUS owners had a great backstory, and it seemed likely more would be revealed with additional digging. Their connections to the village were deep, stakeholders in a wide array of local institutions, from the Church of the Messiah to the Woods Hole Yacht Club, or engaged in the mundane occupations that keep a village humming along. I was anxious to get to know each of them better.

Understanding who else had lived in the house remains difficult to answer as so many people have lived in the house over the years. While Walter Nickerson was alive, he and his wife rented out their house on Middle Street to local tradesmen and their families year-round. For a number of years, they also rented part or all of the house on Millfield for the lucrative summer months, during which time Helena would visit her sister Gertrude in Dalton. Untold numbers of professors and students spent summers there, a stone's throw from the world-renowned research labs.

It was more difficult to rent out the big house during the off-season, when temperatures plunged. In fact, Walter and his family relocated to the smaller Middle Street house themselves during the winter of 1919. Even with five fireplaces, the large home on the water must have been a challenge to keep comfortable when nor'easters or Alberta clippers raged. After Walter died, the house was rented regularly in the warmer months as a source of income, though Helena returned to the house during the summer throughout World War II.

When Edward A. Norman purchased the house, it was frequently rented to people affiliated with Woods Hole Oceanographic Institution (WHOI) and Marine Biological Laboratory (MBL). In 1947, he rented the house to Dr. Otto Loewl, a former professor of pharmacology at the University of Graz in Austria.[22] In 1936, Dr. Loewl was awarded the Nobel Prize in Physiology/Medicine, and two years later he was detained by the Nazis. He was released and spent the rest of his life in New York and Woods Hole. It seems rather fitting that he died in New York City while dining on New England lobster, and his ashes are buried in the Woods Hole Cemetery next to his wife's.

In 1950, the "Norman House, formerly called the Nickerson house, [was] leased by the Woods Hole Oceanographic Institution for a summer apartment house and men's dormitory."[23] From that time forward, the house was occupied exclusively by renters, often students or faculty at the scientific institutions. It would be nearly impossible to compile a comprehensive list of all the previous residents, but even today, people we meet recall that they lived in the building or attended parties there many years before, which is a wonderful testament to the house's deep ties to the community.

In 1951, shortly after purchasing the house, Sidney and Josephine Lawrence made several noteworthy changes. The street-facing façade was significantly altered when they removed the front porch, presumably to add an exterior staircase, creating a secondary egress for the apartment. It was quite the spectacle, as "Woods Hole residents were amazed this week to see a porch wheeled on a huge truck out Harbor Hill road to Nobska road. The porch was from Mr. and Mrs. Sidney W. Lawrence's Millfield street home and was being taken to the Lawrence property on Nobska road where it will be converted into a cottage."[24]

The porch can be seen on the 1923 Sanborn map of the property,[25] running the entire length of the house. Full-length porches were common features on hipped-roof Colonial Revival houses at the time, and the house next door still has one. Though not a perfect rendering, the house would have looked similar to the 1900 house, designed by John J. Petit in Brooklyn, New York.[26] The locations of the Palladian window, the entry and the dormer are different, but the features are quite similar. Also included on the 1923 map is the "addition" with the laundry room prominently jutting out toward the water. A quick study of the basement foundation confirms that the extra asymmetrical space facing the water was not an addition but was included at the time the house was originally built.

This Colonial Revival house, designed by John J. Petit in 1900, features a similar full-length porch, Palladian window and hip roof as 22 Millfield. *New York Landmark Preservation Commission.*

Later in 1952, Sidney Lawrence was granted a variance of the town's zoning laws by the Falmouth Board of Appeals, as he "sought a permit to remodel the old Nickerson house on Millfield street, Woods Hole. Mr. Lawrence said this week he intends to remodel the house to provide five apartments. There are two full stories and four or five rooms in the dormers. The dwelling was built during the first World War by Walter Nickerson."[27]

With that newspaper clipping, the answer to question no. 3 was now resolved. For seventy years, since the conversion in 1952, the house has been divided into five or six apartments, rented mostly to WHOI and MBL students and staff. Hundreds of people have lived under its roof during those years. And while it is clear who owned the house throughout its time, there are, no doubt, many interesting people who lived there. Summer people, scientists, students, smart people, party people. In addition to Dr. Loewl, how many other Nobel Prize winners lived in the house?

One thing is certain: Woods Hole attracts a fascinating array of people and has for centuries. This house alone has been owned by a lobstering postman, a millionaire, a road surveyor and two scientists. Others around the village have similarly impressive and eclectic pedigrees. What is it about Woods Hole that captivates such a variety of interesting people, and how will all this talent shape the future?

# BOOK II
# THE VILLAGE

*You need a village if only for the pleasure of leaving it. A village means that you are not alone, knowing that in the people, the trees, the earth, there is something that belongs to you, waiting for you when you are not there.*
—Cesare Pavese

# WELCOME TO WOODS HOLE

D riving into the village of Woods Hole is reminiscent of the opening scene from the movie *Jaws*. The hamlet sits on Vineyard Sound, and the rhythm of life is tied to the coming and going of the Steamship Authority vessels that ferry families, bikes and dogs to Martha's Vineyard year-round. The smell of seafood permeates the air, dominated by the aroma of clam chowder and scrod, with the not-so-subtle undertones of boiled lobster and fried calamari. The greedy sounds of gulls resonate as they fly about, looking for an easy meal at the water's edge.

In the summer, the streets are filled with people enjoying ice cream, shopping for sweatshirts and racing for the ferry. The population of Woods Hole swells to 3,500 during the summer, as top research scientists in oceanography and marine science from around the world gather to study and collaborate. There is a biennial model boat show in late spring; a film festival in early August; and later that month, the famous Falmouth Road Race, which started in 1973 as a seven-mile bar-to-bar run, from the Captain Kidd restaurant in Woods Hole to The Brothers 4 club (now the restaurant Shipwrecked) in Falmouth Heights.

The classic July Fourth parade features marching scientists, doctoral candidates, young future researchers from the Children's School of Science and local business owners. In recent years, the parade included "Social Scientists" (wearing lab coats and sipping from martini glasses), a lobster-clad restaurateur, and—emulating a Chinese dragon in a Lunar New Year parade—a fifty-foot-long guinea worm made of bamboo segments,

Local July 4 parade in Woods Hole, 2018. Led by local fife and drum ensemble, the parade highlights science, patriotism and humor. *Sheehy Collection*.

celebrating the worldwide eradication of this scourge. No politics, no controversy, just very creative fun!

In the off-season, the population drops to 850, but the culture of Woods Hole is no less vibrant. Throughout the cooler months, there are lectures at the Marine Biological Laboratory and Woods Hole Oceanographic Institution better known by their acronyms, MBL and WHOI, as well as book events at the Woods Hole Library and historical talks at the Woods Hole Historical Museum. Liberty Hall, the community center on Water Street, hosts concerts and folk dancing, and restaurants stay open most months, though on a limited schedule.

One hundred years ago, village life was not dramatically different. The ferries took well-to-do families to their summer homes on Martha's Vineyard and Nantucket; many vacationers arrived at the ferry terminal by train from Boston and New York. Train service to Woods Hole was discontinued in 1964, and the railbeds were repurposed into the Shining Sea Bikeway in 1975. The Steamship Authority discontinued the Woods Hole–Nantucket ferry run in 1986, shifting the Nantucket route exclusively to Hyannis. While some people simply viewed Woods Hole as a transit point to the islands, the uber-wealthy found a haven in the grand homes on Penzance Point and the uber-educated in the state-of-the-art laboratories at MBL and WHOI. But even in the years before the establishment of Woods Hole as a mecca of ocean studies and summertime frolicking, the village was home to hardworking and determined families.

Since Bartholomew Gosnold first landed in the area in 1602, Woods Hole has continually, and successfully, reinvented itself as the economic times required. In 1679, fourteen settlers purchased land in the town of Falmouth—then called Succonessett—from the Wampanoag Indians, establishing Woods Hole as one of eight villages in Falmouth. For the next century, very little changed in the lifestyle of the inhabitants. By 1790, the population had grown to a whopping seventy-five men, women and children, who were occupied with farming, fishing and breeding sheep. It was a quiet life, though not without unpleasant odors, thanks to the fish and the livestock.

Over the next 70 years, the economy transitioned dramatically, away from the small farms and toward the sea, first through the rise of whaling and then with the manufacturing of fish-based fertilizer. In the early 1800s, the emergence of the whaling industry changed the economic fortunes of the sleepy fishing village. Since the eighteenth century, whaling had been a mainstay economy on the island of Nantucket, located about twenty-five miles south of Cape Cod, at a time when whales were so plentiful they could be spotted from the island's lookout "masts" erected along the southern shore. Following the Revolutionary War, demand for whale products spiked throughout the country as Americans discovered innumerable uses for whale products. The skilled Nantucket whalers quickly depleted the whale populations in New England, and they found it profitable to embark on yearslong voyages around the world, chasing these enormous mammals on ever-larger ships. Unfortunately, the mouth of Nantucket Harbor was notoriously shallow, made worse by silting, and after a time, these larger ships had difficulty entering and leaving port.[28] Whaling ship captains sought a more convenient location to bring their product to market. Some shifted to New Bedford, but others headed to Woods Hole.

The deep harbor at Bar Neck Wharf in Woods Hole was an ideal spot for whaling ships from around the globe to dock. Throughout the village, businesses were established to support the large ships. The wharf area bustled with activity. Shops sprang up to outfit the ships with supplies, including barrel-coopers, blacksmiths and a bake house that made the hard, dry crackers called hardtack, crucial on long sea voyages.

Whale processing industries dominated the village. The Candle House, built in 1836 on Water Street, was the center for producing spermaceti candles, and today, it is the last remnant of the whaling industry in Woods Hole. The candles were made from the waxy substance found in the head cavity of sperm whales. It required high heat to extract the wax from the sperm oil, and the thick stone walls of the Candle House protected the village from potential accidents. For more than half a century, processing whale blubber was a lucrative, albeit smelly, endeavor in the village.

In addition to kitting the ships and processing the catch, the talented maritime craftsmen at the Bar Neck shipyard, located where WHOI now resides, built a number of whaling ships. The *Commodore Morris*, immortalized in a painting by Franklin L. Gifford that hangs in the Woods Hole Library, was built there in 1841. The design of the *Commodore Morris* is nearly identical to that of the *Charles W. Morgan*, built that same year in New Bedford and now serving as a museum ship at Mystic Seaport, the only surviving wooden whaling ship in the world. As the "twin" ship of the *Commodore Morris*, the *Charles W. Morgan*'s bow was replicated in miniature in the 1960s by Robert Hampton, head of the MBL's boat shop, and graces the front of the Candle House today.[29]

Many coastal communities were caught unprepared when whaling became less profitable in the late 1850s. Until then, American whalers had an economic edge over their global competition, with faster, better ships and abundant cheap labor. In New Bedford, which was the center of whaling in New England and at one point the richest city per capita in the country, jobs began shifting to manufacturing, driving up labor costs and making it easier for other nations to compete on the seas. In addition, demand for whale products declined with the introduction of kerosene lamps, which used petroleum-based oil, eliminating the need for the dirtier, smellier whale oil in homes and businesses. By the end of the century, the whaling industry had died, and Nantucket's fortunes died with it.

Though it had come to rely heavily on whaling, Woods Hole did not suffer the same fate as Nantucket. The booming whaling industry inspired a focus on infrastructure that served the village well as it reinvented itself following these economic changes. Whaling required the movement of goods to and from ships, and Falmouth invested in better roads and a bridge over the outlet for Eel Pond to transport goods more efficiently. This laid the groundwork for the successful transition to other economic ventures, ensuring the village's continued prosperity. Fortunately, the same deep-water harbor that made Woods Hole ideal for whaling ships, with improved roads around the area, also made it an ideal port for a new and similarly pungent business.

*Top*: Manufacturing center for spermaceti candles in Woods Hole, 1893. The stone Candle House (*right*) connects to the tryhouse, where whale oil was heated to dangerously high temperatures for processing. *WHHM*.

*Bottom*: Franklin L. Gifford's painting of the whaling ship Commodore Morris, which was built in Woods Hole in 1841 and owned by Oliver Swift. *Woods Hole Public Library*.

# Fertilizer!

In the mid-nineteenth century, with cities filling up with immigrants fleeing famine and persecution in Europe, the U.S. government actively sought to expand its population into the plains of the Midwest. "Manifest Destiny, a phrase coined in 1845, is the idea that the United States is destined—by God, its advocates believed—to expand its dominion and spread democracy and capitalism across the entire North American continent."[30] The Louisiana Purchase in 1803 was the first major territory expansion, followed by the annexation of Texas (1845), the acquisition of the Oregon Territory from Britain (1846) and the ceding of Mexican Territory following the Mexican American War (1848), securing land coast-to-coast that the government was anxious to see settled. The United States had plentiful land for farming and spreading out, unlike the crowded conditions in Europe at the time. The population of the United States exploded through immigration and a high birth rate, quadrupling from 5 million in 1800 to 23 million by 1850.[31] The gold rush in 1849 focused on the West Coast, but many of the early pioneers became midwestern farmers. Large farms required high-quality fertilizer to maintain the integrity of the loamy soil, and Woods Hole found a new industry to exploit.

The Pacific Guano Company was started in 1859, a perfect example of Yankee ingenuity leveraging local resources. With the decline of whaling, Woods Hole's deep harbors were available for a new customer. The Cape Cod entrepreneurs who founded the company adapted locally built clipper ships, made obsolete by the expansion of railroads for transporting goods between the East and West Coast, to harvest the recently discovered nutrient-rich guano—bird poop—found on islands in the Pacific Ocean. It was a new gold rush of sorts, and the exceedingly fast clipper ships gave the Pacific Guano Company a distinct advantage. With that, it brought a new and especially smelly industry to the village.[32]

The Pacific Guano Company was formed by the Crowell and Shiverick families, established Cape Cod shipbuilders, in partnership with Boston businessmen, with a boost from the U.S. government. Recognizing the importance of the nutrient-rich guano to its expansion goals, and looking to avoid the high prices charged by South American countries for this critical resource, Congress passed the U.S. Guano Act of 1856, authorizing U.S. citizens to lay claim to uninhabited guano islands anywhere in the world and directing the U.S. Navy to support such claims. At its peak, the company had two hundred workers in the Woods Hole factory, running over two dozen

Pacific Guano Company factory on Bar Neck, with locally built clipper ships awaiting cargo. *WHHM.*

clipper ships to its guano islands. The growth contributed to an influx of immigrants from Ireland and the Cape Verde Islands, many of whom settled on Millfield Street. Imagine the smells that must have permeated the area of Bar Neck Harbor, with bird poop odors mingling with rotting, locally caught menhaden fish, thrown into sacks and carted down to the wharf. For better or worse, the factory and its scents did not stick around for long.

*6*

# SCIENTISTS AND SUMMER PEOPLE

In 1872, the commercial viability of Woods Hole transformed with the arrival of the railroad. The Old Colony Railroad, which ran lines along southeastern Massachusetts and Rhode Island, was convinced to extend its line to the village through the combined effort of Prince Sears Crowell, one of the founders of the Pacific Guano Company; financier John Murray Forbes of Naushon Island; and Joseph Story Fay, considered Woods Hole's first summer resident.

Crowell, of course, wanted the railroad for commercial purposes, to transport fertilizer from his factory to major depots across the country, while Forbes was looking for an easy way for his well-to-do family and close friends to journey to his retreat offshore. Since 1842, when Forbes purchased Naushon Island, which lies just south of Woods Hole, the island has served as a relaxing and private enclave for the family. Guests were ferried to the island from the village, and arriving dockside in a private railroad coach was certainly preferable to rattling along the dusty roads in a horse-drawn carriage.

Joseph Story Fay had a more altruistic interest for championing railroad service. Fay and his family discovered Woods Hole in the 1850s on a trip to Cape Cod, and they were smitten by it. They abandoned their plans to vacation elsewhere and instead purchased a home in Woods Hole for use in the summer months. Recognizing that Woods Hole was a special place, and that others might share his passion for healthy air, wholesome residents and inspiring views, Joseph Story Fay bought up

Oil painting by Frank Hill Smith, 1876. *Lady in Hammock* portrays Elizabeth Eliot Spooner Fay (1851–1945) enjoying summer's slower pace. She was the wife of Henry H. Fay, who sold the property on Eel Pond to Walter E. Nickerson in 1913. *WHHM*.

a significant amount of undeveloped land in the area. Fay envisioned an idyllic village, wholesome and prosperous, and over time he donated much of his land to advance his vision. In 1852, he donated three acres of land to build the Church of the Messiah, the first Episcopal church on Cape Cod. Thirty-five years later, he offered funds to replace the wooden building with the current stone church. A deeply religious man, he felt it was important for the newly arrived—and fairly poor—Irish and Portuguese factory workers to have a place to worship, so he donated the land on which St. Joseph's Catholic Church was erected on Millfield Street in 1881.[33]

Fay's commitment to shaping community life went well beyond his religious efforts. In the 1860s, understanding the myriad benefits a good transportation system could provide, he donated the land on which the railroad extension was built. In addition to moving fertilizer, the trains brought people to the ferries heading to the islands, and they also moved fresh fish from Sam Cahoon's Woods Hole Fish Market up to Boston. These activities brought prosperity to Woods Hole and laid the groundwork for future success.

When the Pacific Guano Company, saddled with $2 million in debt and suggestions of malfeasance, went bankrupt in 1889 and its manufacturing plant disappeared, the village could have suffered a catastrophic economic setback. Fortunately, the railroad depot remained. It did not take long for both the factory's land at the edge of town and the trains that carted its product to market to be repurposed and for Woods Hole to reinvent itself yet again. The land around the industrial wharf was scooped up by scientists, while the formerly stinky peninsula of Bar Neck was transformed into an exclusive enclave of summer homes for the very wealthy.

The scientists, who started arriving in Woods Hole two decades before the factory's demise, were the first to see the potential of the area and were not deterred by the stench. After all, they studied oceans, and the scent of low tide was just an occupational hazard. By the time the fertilizer business collapsed, marine biologists had already primed the pump to secure government commitment and funding for their research.

Interest in marine studies dated back several decades, as the federal government struggled to keep up with the country's rapid growth. In the latter half of the nineteenth century, as the population exploded along the East Coast with the influx of immigrants into New York and Boston, there was a rising concern in government circles about the potential depletion of fish stocks that were crucial to feeding the nation. In 1871, President Ulysses Grant signed a bill creating the independent Office of Commissioner of Fish and Fisheries, focused on the study of "the decrease of the food fishes of the seacoasts and lakes of the United States, and to suggest remedial measures." Headquarters were established at Woods Hole, not far from where whaling ships had been built a half century earlier, and where the water, kept clean and clear by the strong currents, was ideal for researching striped bass, bluefish and other species. The focus of the nascent commission was on biological research, but efforts were also made to establish a hatchery. An aquarium was set up at this time, one of the earliest in the United States.[34]

With the establishment of a permanent laboratory for biological research in 1875, other scientists were attracted to Woods Hole. In 1888, the Marine Biological Laboratory (MBL) was established, with its emphasis on both research and teaching. Scientists were beginning to understand that the same "essential processes of life, such as cell division, nerve and muscle activity, and development, might be studied more easily in simple marine forms than in higher animals."[35] In other words, researchers could learn a great deal about the human body by studying plankton and jellyfish. The deep harbor allowed research vessels to dock, and vast quantities of specimens could be collected from the local waters for study.

In the early years, women were welcome to participate in the scientific coursework offered at MBL. In fact, from 1888 to 1910, women made up about a third of the students and researchers attending its summer program. In some classes, such as Botany and Embryology, they accounted for half the enrollment. Many of these women taught in secondary schools, so these summer courses offered insights that would trickle down to classrooms across the country. Women were instrumental in raising funds to establish the MBL, and for many years they were admitted on an equal footing with men. The enrollment of women declined after 1910 and did not pick up again until the 1970s.[36]

It was during the period of declining female attendance that Rachel Carson became a celebrated scientific writer in Woods Hole. Raised on

Many local "non-scientists" were paid to collect marine specimens for the labs during the summer months. *WHHM.*

a family farm in Pennsylvania, she published her first story in *St. Nicholas Magazine* at the tender age of ten. Rachel Carson possessed the unusual combination of literary talent and a passion for biology, earning a master's degree in zoology in 1932. She faced a number of personal challenges; the most urgent was supporting her ailing family members during the Great Depression. She secured a position in Woods Hole with the U.S. Bureau of Fisheries, first writing radio scripts and then brochures and informational documents for public consumption. Her most famous work, *Silent Spring* (1962), bolstered the movement to ban DDT use in the United States and influenced the establishment of the Environmental Protection Agency. Rachel Carson died at the age of fifty-six following a long battle with breast cancer. A statue of her likeness gazes out on Vineyard Sound from a bench near the U.S. Fisheries building in Woods Hole.

The Woods Hole Oceanographic Institution (WHOI) was established in 1930, with its focus on ocean science and marine engineering. For several decades, these scientific communities operated only in the summer, and then—as now—their participants added significant numbers to the summer population of the village. The relaxed atmosphere provided welcome respite from the intensely competitive university environment experienced during the academic year, and it promoted creative and collaborative thinking. It also encouraged these cerebral experts to let loose.

Every year the studious and brilliant students looked forward to the Men vs. Girls baseball game, when the men would dress up in women's clothes and take to the baseball diamond. There were clambakes at Tarpaulin Cove as they collected marine specimens on the beach, singalongs and other lighthearted activities.[37] Nowadays, the students celebrate the end of summer with creative races featuring homemade boats at Stoney Beach.

The scientific community has thrived in Woods Hole, making it a premier clearinghouse for knowledge on marine biology, oceanography and climate issues. It is the home port of the most advanced research vessels in the world, operated by WHOI in partnership with the U.S. Navy. Though relatively small in size, the reach of the community is global, and its impact is beyond measure. Even as it gathers data to better understand the implications of climate issues on a global scale, including the threat of rising oceans, the local community in Woods Hole is applying that information to protect its own assets, millions of dollars in sophisticated laboratory equipment that sits in facilities just a few feet above sea level, as well as locally owned homes and businesses.

*Top*: The annual Men versus Girls baseball game played in Woods Hole Park. *WHHM*.

*Bottom*: Summertime 1920s fashion on display at Stoney Beach. *WHHM*.

*Opposite*: Silly scientists (men and women) enjoying the relaxed summer atmosphere on the docks near the MBL. *WHHM*.

As Woods Hole transitioned from factory to laboratory, Falmouth Heights was actively reinventing itself as a summer resort. Just four miles north of Woods Hole, Falmouth was, historically, a town full of mariners. The decline of whaling hit the town hard, as did the nationwide shift from ships to trains for transporting goods, and for several decades its economic fortunes declined. Falmouth did not have the benefit of steady revenue that the Pacific Guano Factory brought to Woods Hole, but it also wasn't sullied by the grit and unpleasant smells of an industrial zone. Interest in seaside towns was a rising phenomenon throughout the nineteenth century, and by the time the railroad arrived in 1871, Falmouth was poised for an economic lift.

Early on, only wealthy Bostonians could afford the cost of building and maintaining summer homes, and during this period, a few families, including the Fays and the Beebes, bought up vast tracts of land in the area. It was the arrival of daily rail service that created an opportunity for summer retreats for the less affluent and transformed the Falmouth economy. Reliable train service offered convenience for Boston—and even New York—families to escape the heat of the city, and they happily adopted the less formal lifestyle of Cape Cod, enjoying the healthy air and cool ocean breezes. Women in long dresses, fancy hats and parasols would promenade along the beaches from May through September. Small summer homes grew up along the shore roads, along with the enormous "cottages" of the very wealthy, and Falmouth flourished.

With its commercial activity, Woods Hole was known as a working village, not a resort. Fishing boats landed their catch, while shipments of processed fertilizer were carted down to the railroad for transport. Scientists and their assistants were digging in the tidal muck for specimens to study. It was a noisy and malodorous spot, hardly the setting for summer visitors. The only reason for most summer people to go to Woods Hole was to catch a boat to the islands.

All that changed when the Pacific Guano Company closed. By 1892, the land on Bar Neck, where the factory buildings had stood, was sold to Horace C. Crowell and William Nye and subdivided into twenty-four large estates. The spot was renamed Penzance Point and featured a single road that ran down the center of the u-shaped peninsula. Crowell had prearranged the sales of these plots to wealthy industrialists within his social circle, creating a casual "anti-city" version of their socially rigid metropolitan life.

Within a few years, Penzance Point was dotted with enormous homes, most of them designed to take advantage of the narrow spit of land to catch breezes coming from both Vineyard Sound and Buzzards Bay. Unlike the fancy homes in Newport, these houses were built for relaxing with family and close friends, an escape from the formality and social rules that city life demanded. These large estates also had the benefit of privacy, which was lacking in Falmouth, where even the large homes were nestled close to their neighbors. By 1900, Woods Hole had completely transformed from a factory town to a summer destination, with the railroad bringing throngs of people to catch the ferries to the islands, to study at the marine laboratories or to rent a cottage for a few weeks of recreation in the village of Woods Hole.

One additional transition speaks to Woods Hole's resilience and highlights the symbiotic relationship between summer people and locals. In 1898, Henry H. Fay, along with other like-minded summer residents, drew up a charter for a golf club, making it the second-oldest private golf club on Cape Cod, bested only by the Cummaquid Golf Club in Yarmouth Port, founded three years previously. The incorporated group initially leased land from the Fay estate, opening the Woods Hole Golf Club in 1899. For several years, local residents were kept employed removing large rocks, known as erratics, from the fairways.

Cape Cod formed around twenty thousand years ago, as glaciers pushed their way south during the last ice age. As the glacier moved south, it dislodged granite in its path, and the loosened rocks formed the leading edge of the glacier. When the glacier retreated around eighteen thousand years ago, it left behind rock, clay and blocks of ice. The ice became imbedded in sediment, and when it melted, the empty space filled with water, forming the kettle ponds found throughout the Cape. Rocks that had been picked up hundreds of miles to the north in the White Mountains of New Hampshire were left unceremoniously along the glacier's southernmost edge, very much like seaweed is left to mark the high tide point on a beach. These rocks have no geological commonalities with the surrounding native rock and are called erratics. It was a colossal task to remove them, and even today many of the massive boulders fringe the golf course's edge.

The course initiation fee was fifty dollars, and by 1900 the club had sixty-four members. The early clubhouse was a simple affair with stunning views of Buzzard's Bay and Quissett Harbor. Upon the course's opening, the newspaper described that "situated on the very top of the highest point of land in the locality is the cosey clubhouse of the Woods Hole Golf Club, where no matter from which direction the wind may blow, a cooling breeze

*Top*: The upgraded clubhouse of the Woods Hole Golf Club, built in 1921. *Woods Hole Golf Club.*

*Bottom*: Woods Hole Golf Club's caddy camp in 1929. *Woods Hole Golf Club.*

is sure to sweep across the veranda, adding much to the pleasure of watching the players go over the course."[38]

When the club members purchased the Fay property outright in 1916, they proceeded to build a much larger and grander clubhouse. In 1929, the club founded a caddy camp, training over fifty caddies that first summer, and becoming one of the finest caddy training sites in the country. Campers lived in tents on the current site of the fifteenth fairway, until cabins were built following a bout of leaking tents. For the most part, the Woods Hole Golf Club was the playground of the elite summer residents.[39]

In the postwar years, club operations declined. The caddy club closed in 1953; the cabins fell into disrepair and were demolished in 1964. Incredibly, it was the townspeople who came to the rescue and saved the golf club. As recounted in the WHHM archives, "In the early 1950's, club membership had declined to less than 100. Both the clubhouse and course were in need of extensive maintenance. According to Dutch Wessner, 'There just wasn't enough money to support the club.' It was the local members—those with the least money—who saved the course. These members realized that in order for the club to survive, it had to reach out for new members beyond Woods Hole's summer residents, to its year-round residents and other Cape Codders. Fundraising efforts included many social activities and golf tournaments open to non-members. These activities piqued the interest of townspeople, summer residents, and retirees. Membership grew and money came in. There has been a long waiting list for membership for many years. The volunteer efforts of new members and the influx of funds allowed the needed renovations to be completed. The community spirit which was engendered during these growth years continues to this day."[40]

The survival of the WHGC relied on the creative thinking of both local and summer members, who recognized the value of the club to the greater community, identified the challenge (not enough wealthy summer residents to support the club), and came up with a simple and clever solution. They opened up the facility to those who had been excluded in the past, broadening the member base and ensuring a future for the entire association. The established club members adapted to the rather significant change of welcoming members outside their familiar circles, and as a result the Woods Hole Golf Club rebounded, becoming the top-tier golf club that it remains to this day. Its ongoing success depends on the summer residents, the local year-round golfers and even the support of non-golfers who appreciate the beautiful green space in the center of Woods Hole. In many ways, the evolution of the WHGC encapsulates those characteristics that make Woods Hole such a special—and enduring—place.

7

# Nobska Lighthouse and Its Keeper

Woods Hole lays claim to many iconic symbols. The village is home to some of the best-known acronyms in science, including WHOI (Woods Hole Oceanographic Institution), MBL (Marine Biological Laboratory) and NOAA (National Oceanic and Atmospheric Administration). Woods Hole is also the terminus for the Steamship Authority ferry to Martha's Vineyard, the starting point of the Falmouth Road Race and home to the Woods Hole Golf Club. That's a whole lot of "famous" for a place with a population of 850.

But the ultimate iconic symbol of Woods Hole—and Falmouth, for that matter—is the lighthouse at Nobska Point. Its image graces any number of official websites, T-shirts and coffee mugs. Beginning with its establishment in 1828, when it was known as "Nobsque Light," the lighthouse played a critical role in Woods Hole's growth, aiding safe passage through challenging waters. At the beginning of the nineteenth century, when Nantucket was a major whaling center, Woods Hole's deep harbor made it a perfect partner as a mainland processing point. Ships traveling between Boston and New York added to the congestion. According to the Cuttyhunk Historical Society, Vineyard Sound was considered the "world's second busiest shipping passage (after the English Channel) and one of the most dangerous."[41] The waters off Woods Hole are full of shallow ledges, treacherous shoals and extremely strong currents, at times exceeding four and a half knots, challenging the navigation skills of even the most experienced seaman. The increased maritime traffic around Woods Hole,

The newly restored Nobska Lighthouse now offers a museum open to the public. *Sheehy Collection*.

and the approximately ten thousand vessels that passed through Vineyard Sound each year, convinced Congress to appropriate $3,000 to build a lighthouse on four acres of land at Nobska Point.

The first lighthouse "was in the typical Cape-Cod style, with an octagonal tower atop a stone keeper's house, with three rooms on the first floor and two small rooms upstairs. The lantern room held 10 lamps with 14-inch reflectors producing a fixed white light 78 feet above the sea."[42] In 1874, Oliver A. Nickerson was appointed lighthouse keeper, moving his growing family into the stone house. He went on to become the longest-serving keeper at Nobska, working up to the moment of his death in 1911. Though he died before the house on Millfield was even built, he proved to be a critical link in its heritage as the father of Walter E. Nickerson.

Oliver's journey to Nobska Point was a bit rocky at times, and it's a wonder he rose to such success in his career, considering he was brought before a grand jury on murder charges early in his life. As they say, all's well that ends well.

The first "Nobsque" Light, built in 1828, featured a tower atop a stone house, which leaked whenever it rained. It was replaced in 1875. *WHHM.*

Oliver Arey Nickerson was born in Chatham, Massachusetts, in 1836. Both he and his wife were direct descendants of William and Anne (Busby) Nickerson, who established a farm in Monomoyick (later Chatham) in 1656. Their descendants on Cape Cod and the Islands are many, and the name Nickerson remains a venerable one to this day.

Young Oliver went to sea at twenty-two as a cook on the fishing schooner *Fillmore*, an unremarkable vocation if not for the dramatic occurrence on July 1, 1859. While the *Fillmore* lay in port at Gabarus, Nova Scotia, one of its crew members, Albert Day, went missing, showing up dead several days later.[43]

The story was an international sensation, framed by the *Barnstable Patriot* as "the death by violence and treachery, at Gabarus, of a stranger named Alfred Day."[44] The paper reported that "several of the crew were with the deceased on shore on Friday night, drinking and quarreling. They repaired to the vessel about 2 o'clock, leaving Day still on shore. Shortly afterwards a man named Bagnell, accompanied Day to the beach, and saw him safe aboard a boat bound to join the schooner. On Saturday morning a report was abroad that the deceased was missing—the boat having been found on the beach, to which she appeared to have drifted."[45]

Suspicion rose among the Cape Bretons when the schooner set sail the following day after a brief but unsuccessful search for the missing crew member. Day's body was finally found the following Tuesday with a broken nose, cut mouth and "mortal wound" on his temple. The *Cape Breton News* reported that "an inquest was held…and the verdict of wilful [*sic*] murder returned."[46] The reporting placed blame for the death squarely on the crew of the *Fillmore*, one of whom presumably murdered him while he slept.

Outside of Gabarus, this theory was met with skepticism. Day had been "left on shore by the crew in a locality that is [notoriously] of riotous and disorderly character."[47] The *Patriot* suggested that Bagnell, a local—and the last man known to see Day alive—should have been arrested.

The *Fillmore* continued to fish in Georges Bank but cut short its voyage, returning to Cape Cod on September 12. Even in 1859, with the ship miles out to sea, public opinion affected these sailors. Without phones or the internet, word of the sensational murder in Nova Scotia traveled through the fishing community around Georges Bank, as ships used speaking trumpets and semaphore, a series of color-coded flags, to communicate with each other while at sea. News from back home would be passed along from ship to ship—even between whaling ships out in the Pacific—keeping the crew up to date on births, deaths and especially scandal.

Increasingly, the crew felt the judgment of their peers, the insinuation of a cover-up, and they urgently desired to clear their names. Captain and crew were confident that the truth would prevail when they turned back early for Yarmouth to submit to examination by the authorities, putting full faith in the justice system. It is not inconceivable that modern-day reporters would have pounced on the dramatic storyline, and the outcome could have been a much messier affair.[48]

Upon arriving in Yarmouth, "Oliver A. Nickerson, cook of the fishing [schooner] *Fillmore*, was brought before U.S. Commissioner, H.L. Hallet, charged with assault with a dangerous weapon upon Alfred Day, one of the crew of said schooner." Questioning of the witnesses soon followed, and the accounts of the crew members was consistent throughout. Ephraim P. Steel, skipper of the *Fillmore*, testified that he last saw Alfred Day at seven or eight o'clock in the evening, at which time he had been "quite sober," which was notable, as both Day and Nickerson had been intoxicated earlier in the afternoon while ashore. Steel said he headed back to the Fillmore at ten o'clock, with crewmembers Nickerson, Kent and Burgess, and all hands turned in. Day did not come aboard with them and reportedly was headed to the store of a Mr. Nicholson.[49]

The next morning, Steel "inquired for Day and was told he had not come on board. Afterwards [I] saw the dory which had been left for him, on the rocks ashore. Supposed he was drowned. Went ashore and made some inquiries and then proceeded to sea, as I had before intended to do. Went out 4 or 5 miles, and concluded to go back to see if we could get more news of Day, or ship another hand. The crew was subsequently examined before a magistrate and discharged."[50]

E.E. Kent, the ship's boy, while giving Oliver a strong alibi (they shared a cabin), let slip that Day and Nickerson had gotten drunk earlier in the day and Nickerson "threatened to kill" Day, though they made up later, once sober. This narrative of reconciliation was confirmed by other witnesses, and Captain Steel himself testified that no one on his crew was culpable. At this point, the prosecution rested.

George A. King, Esq., mounted a straightforward defense, stressing that their presence in court was proof of the crew's innocence. "They had heard, while at sea, of the reports current respecting them in connection with this affair, and like men conscious of having committed no wrong, they had left their voyage uncompleted and come home to meet these accusations." King suggested that "all the evidence tends that Day got drunk on shore, got into difficulty there, and was killed. To hide the crime, the body of Day was probably carried and dropped where it was found, by those who perpetrated it.…The whole case rested upon the idle threats of a drunken man."[51]

The case was remanded to the U.S. District Court in Boston, and within a week a grand jury considered the matter and dismissed the case. Oliver Nickerson was a free man. The *Yarmouth Register* editorialized, "We are glad that justice has been done to Nickerson and his shipmates, for it is evident upon the testimony in the case, that they are all entirely innocent of the crime which some have unjustly suspected they committed."[52]

Beyond the drama, one cannot help but be impressed by the efficacy of the judicial system in 1859. The murder took place five hundred miles from the courthouse, in another country no less, yet there was a process in place to expedite the examination of witnesses, quickly remanding the case to a higher court and then efficiently concluding there was no cause for further action. From the arrival of the crew in Yarmouth on September 12 to the conclusion of the matter on September 19, the case took only one week in the courts. Needless to say, such a notorious case would not be so easily adjudicated today.

It is not clear whether Bagnell or anyone else was ever held accountable for the death of Alfred Day, but Oliver returned to his family in Chatham and lived a relatively quiet life for the next fifty years. He married a very distant cousin, Mary Elizabeth Nickerson, in 1857. Their first child, Vesta "Betsy" C. Nickerson, was born in 1858 and would be joined by eight siblings (Walter was the middle child) over the next twenty years. Oliver earned a living from the sea, listing his occupation variously as a seaman, mariner or boatman, before settling into his role of keeper. As noted in his obituary in the *Falmouth Enterprise*, "Captain Nickerson was in the employ of the government for many years....He served as captain on several lightships."[53]

In 1874, shortly after arriving at Nobska Point, Mary gave birth to her eighth child, Florence Imogene Nickerson, in the old stone keeper's house. The forty-six-year-old structure was not an ideal environment for a family of ten (youngest son Herman R. Nickerson was born in 1878). With the light tower jutting through the roof of the house, wind and weather had taken a toll, as the "weight of the eight-foot in diameter tower topped by an octagonal iron lantern put severe stress on the dwelling's roof, and ultimately on the keepers and their families. Several tenants complained that when it rained the entire family was forced to maneuver their beds to avoid the leaks."[54]

In 1875, in an effort to modernize the lighthouse system, a "fog bell sounded by machinery was established at Nobska Point."[55] While on site, the Lighthouse Board, which had oversight of operations, noted the dilapidated state of the existing lighthouse station. The following year, the Nobska Light complex was completely replaced. A forty-foot-tall cast-iron tower, manufactured at a foundry in Chelsea, Massachusetts, and lined with brick, was erected, along with a new two-story keeper's house. With six private rooms, this structure was much better suited for a family, and over the years the Nickersons frequently welcomed guests to stay at their home with its sweeping views of Vineyard Sound.

Improvements to the Nobska Lighthouse station continued. In December 1887, the 1856 fifth-order Fresnel lens was replaced with a larger fourth-order Fresnel lens, which remains in use today, along with "a red sector to mark dangerous shoals in the area. A covered walkway connecting the tower to the keeper's house was added in 1899." In 1905, a second dwelling was added to the site to serve as the assistant keeper's house, a position added in 1910.[56]

One of the tasks of lighthouse keepers was tracking maritime traffic that passed through the area, recording it by type (ships, brigs, schooners, sloops,

NOBSQUE . 1895 . 7677.

Nobska Light as it looked in 1895 before an assistant keeper's house was added to the complex. *WHHM.*

etc.) in a *Journal of Vessels* and submitting it monthly. During the final years of Oliver Nickerson's tenure, his youngest daughter, Florence, who never married, took on the task of recording these vessels. She was described in a 1908 article as "shrewd and kindly, one of those Yankee girls who fear nothing and take life cheerfully."[57] During this time, she served as an unpaid assistant to her father, who was well into his seventies.

In 1910, a number of changes came to Nobska Point that affected both the family and the village. The Lighthouse Board, still concerned about foggy conditions, planned "to install a steam fog whistle at Nobska Point. Summer residents objected to the plan on grounds that it was unnecessary and would reduce the value of their property,"[58] presumably because of the jarring noise of the horn. Those with shipping interests responded that "no local interests, however influential, should be permitted to deter your honorable Board from giving the fullest possible protection to the great amount of traffic that daily uses this highway of commerce."[59] In the end, the proponents for maritime safety prevailed, and a brick fog signal building, known as the whistle house, was built and equipped to sound the warning when visibility dropped below five miles.

One hundred years later, the locals continue to complain about the foghorn. First, the U.S. Coast Guard moved the foghorn away from the road out of concern for drivers' safety, due to complaints that the loud blast unnerved drivers going past it on foggy days. The double blast every minute at the hairpin turn at Nobska Point caused drivers to lose control of their vehicles in a dangerous spot. In 2020, the fog horn was upgraded by the U.S. Coast Guard to an on-demand system, using the Mariner Radio Activated Sound System (MRASS), which allows passing vessels to activate the foghorn when needed. The foghorn blasts every minute for sixty minutes per activation. Though it is called into service occasionally, the horn is heard less frequently and the duration is usually brief. Some residents miss the mournful sound of the horn, which regularly punctuated a foggy night.

With the installation of the foghorn came a new position at Nobska Point. Though his time at Nobska would be brief—and like Woods Hole, quite rocky—things started calmly enough for the first assistant keeper, George Irving Cameron. Shortly after his arrival in 1910, his wife gave birth to twin boys, and the family of seven settled into the newly built assistant keeper's house.

One year later, though, things started to fall apart when his boss died on the job, and George himself found the dead keeper's body. On May 13, 1911, "Captain Nickerson was apparently as well as usual. After eating breakfast, he walked down to the whistle house [to relieve George Cameron], and shortly after, when the fog cleared away, he shut down the apparatus. When found by George Cameron, the assistant keeper, he was sitting in his accustomed place in the whistle house, apparently asleep. Death was due to heart failure."[60] Oliver Nickerson was seventy-four years old and had served as the keeper at Nobska for thirty-seven years. He is buried in the family plot next to the Church of the Messiah in the village cemetery.

In his obituary, Oliver was described thus: "Captain Nickerson was of a retiring disposition and a man who attended strictly to his own affairs. Aside from an occasional visit to his old home in Chatham, he scarcely left the reservation."[61] The drama of his earlier brush with the law, the serious charge of murder that went before a grand jury and his subsequent exoneration were distant memories and may explain his "retiring disposition" in later life.

In June, George Cameron was promoted to head keeper, which should have been a positive step in his career, but the position was linked to a series of unfortunate events. In August of that same year, just a few months into his tenure, drama struck. The Boston-bound steamer *Bunker Hill*, carrying over three hundred passengers, ran aground on a clear, calm night. "[I]f the pilot or captain, whoever was in charge of the steamer, was trying to hit Nobska Lighthouse," wrote a passenger, "he was a very poor shot, as he didn't come within 100 feet of it, and if he was trying to avoid hitting it, he was an equally poor shot, as he had plenty of water in the broad Vineyard sound to escape striking the beacon, the rays of which must have blinded him, as he was running his vessel toward it."[62] Help was summoned by the keeper, and all passengers were safely unloaded. Though the keeper was in no way responsible for this maritime nightmare, it certainly made for a stressful night.

The drama of George Cameron's time at Nobska Light wasn't over yet, but that story is best kept for later. Now it's time to unravel the story of the house on Eel Pond, built by Walter E. Nickerson, son of the longest-serving keeper of Nobska Light.

# BOOK III
# THE PEOPLE

— ◆ —

*All happy families are alike,*
*but every unhappy family is unhappy in its own way.*
—Anna Karenina, *Leo Tolstoy, 1878*

*8*

# THE NICKERSONS OF WOODS HOLE

T he search for information about the house on Eel Pond required proving—and disproving—many reputed details. Months of intensive research led to a few concrete conclusions: in 1916, in partnership with his wife, Helena, Walter E. Nickerson, son of Nobska lightkeeper Oliver A. Nickerson and Mary Nickerson, built a house on Millfield Street in Woods Hole, Massachusetts. WALTER E. NICKERSON. I had a name and a few snippets of information, but not much else. What could be learned about his family? How did he earn a living? Was he really a sea captain, as Mary Ramsbottom had suggested? I clearly needed more help to answer these questions, and that is how I became a member of Ancestry.com.

## AT THE ROOT OF IT ALL

Genealogy, the study of family history, is an ancient scholarship. The family tree of Confucius dates back over 2,500 years, and tracing ancestral lineage in Genesis extends back even further. In America, the 1977 TV series *Roots*, based on Alex Haley's book, triggered an obsession with uncovering one's ancestry, especially within African American communities. Research shed light on the painful history of enslaved families and impoverished immigrants alike, connecting modern scholars to their past. Though these histories often uncovered ugly facts, there remains a certain pride that comes from a long lineage in this country. Even Alexis de Tocqueville noted in 1840 that "you hardly meet an American who does not want to be connected a bit by his birth to the first settlers of the colonies."[63]

Sometimes genealogical research uncovers surprises, though more often it reinforces oral or written family history. My family came to this country from England in the 1960s, crossing the Atlantic not on the *Mayflower* but on the SS *Leonardo da Vinci*, considered a state-of-the-art vessel in its day but a rather quaint way to travel even then. With no need to discover when or how my family arrived in America, I was less inclined than some to jump on the genealogy bandwagon, until Walter E. Nickerson entered my world.

The Nickerson descendants joined the genealogy craze early, inspired by the patriotic fervor that gripped the country after the Civil War, accompanied by renewed interest in our nation's founding. They established one of the largest family associations in the world, with an impressive website and a museum dedicated to documenting all things Nickerson, housed in the Caleb Nickerson homestead in Chatham, Massachusetts. The Nickerson Family Association was founded in 1897 and set out to document the eight or nine generations of Nickersons already settled in the United States.

In the early years of the association, both Oliver and his daughter Florence were solicited by distant Nickerson kin in Chatham for family histories. In one letter, Thomas Small informed his cousin Oliver—in a letter reminiscent of Genesis—that "Shadrach Small Jr. certainly married Betsey J. Nickerson [Oliver's sister], Oliver Nickerson's daughter of Chatham, brother of my grandmother. She lived while he courted her with her Aunt Ruth Zebina Small's wife, a sister to my grandmother Cahoon."[64] Untangling that explanation with the benefit of Ancestry's robust files, one determines that Thomas was the great-nephew of Oliver's father. Keeping track of family ties in 1910, without the benefit of computerized genealogical tools, would have been a challenge, especially when everyone in town was related in some way and many shared the same names.

Genealogy sites like Ancestry offer subscribers digital access to official and unofficial documents; census data; birth, marriage and death certificates; and other evidence of life events collected from public sites and private submissions. Genealogists understand how easily one gets lost in these websites. It is best described as a series of rabbit holes that lead to additional tunnels and occasionally to a dead end. But when the tunnel opens into a treasure chamber of data, it is magic.

Starting with good clues is a huge help (name, places where the person lived, birth year), and finding one bit of information often leads to the next. Until one hits a dead end. Or worse, one starts following the trail of a *different* person with the same name. Yes, I have experienced both scenarios, often.

Fortunately, Walter E. Nickerson was a bit of a homebody. Born in Chatham in 1867, he moved to Woods Hole in 1874 and lived there until his death fifty years later. In the meantime, he got married, raised a son, built a seawall and then erected a house. It helped the research that he was christened Walter, a popular boy's name in 1867 but somewhat less common within the Nickerson family, which instead favored William, Alfred, Oliver and even an Ebenezer or two. Fact-finding through genealogy websites is not a linear process, and there are likely still bits and pieces of Walter's life that have yet to be uncovered. But even a quiet man like Walter left plenty of breadcrumbs.

William Nickerson and his wife, Anne Busby, fled religious persecution in England and arrived in Chatham in 1656, after a brief stay in Salem. For the first two hundred years, the lives of their descendants changed little. The population in the village of Chatham grew slowly, hovering around 2,500 by the start of the Civil War. The men earned a living from the sea, in fishing, shipping and whaling, while the women pulled the heavy load of raising families and keeping things civilized. Forty miles to the west, Woods Hole was similarly slow to change. Until the 1800s, the population remained stagnant and industry was limited to farming and livestock.

Change came rapidly to Woods Hole once the whaling industry took hold in the first half of the nineteenth century, followed by fertilizer production in the second half, and innovation continues to drive the economy to this day. It took a bit longer for such dramatic change to reach Walter E. Nickerson's family, but once they left Chatham in 1874, change came quickly.

Walter's parents, Oliver and Mary, might as well have been heading to the western frontier, so significant was their move from Chatham. Seven generations of Nickersons had lived in Chatham before them, yet once they moved to Nobska Point, they rarely visited their ancestral home. Woods Hole became their center, and that hold would last for generations.

# Closing Out the Century: 1874–1900

The early years in Woods Hole were relatively quiet for Oliver Nickerson's family, as Mary raised their children on the bluff overlooking Vineyard Sound. The lighthouse sits on a cliff edge, so keeping the children safe could not have been easy, and perhaps *quiet* is not the right word for life in the crowded lightkeeper's house. Shortly after they arrived at Nobska, Mary gave birth to Florence and then Herman four years later, bringing the number of children she delivered over a twenty-year period to nine. Remarkably, they all survived to adulthood, and only one died during Mary's lifetime, quite remarkable for the time.

At a young age, the Nickerson boys were taught to handle small boats. First in Chatham and then in Falmouth, they learned to navigate the shoals that lurk beneath the water's surface and to respect the dangerous currents that could carry a boat away from shore with terrifying speed. They attended school until they were old enough to start supporting the family, as was the custom. Boys generally left school out of necessity by age thirteen, and even at the prestigious Lawrence Academy in Falmouth, girls frequently outnumbered the boys, as even some of the brightest male students left school to go to work.

At sixteen years of age, Vesta Nickerson, the oldest child, was essentially a grown woman when the family came to live at Nobska Point. She became a teacher in West Falmouth and in 1881 married Clarence Gifford, descended from another long-established Cape Cod family. Clarence was a carpenter by trade, and he built them a house in Woods Hole on High Street, in the area known as Crow Hill. Their only child, Waldo, was born in 1882. Vesta rarely left Falmouth, but that doesn't mean she wasn't active. She was treasurer of the Sunday School at the Methodist Episcopal Church in West Falmouth for twenty-five years and a member of the Woman's Christian Temperance Union, one of the first organizations of women devoted to social reform and a key driver during the Progressive Era of the early twentieth century.[65]

As Vesta's younger siblings grew up, they found employment in the village after leaving school. Minnie, the second oldest, was a housekeeper, and most of the boys became boatmen, moving product from the ships to the trains, as well as fishing, lobstering and transporting people to the small islands around Woods Hole, depending on the season.

The closing years of the nineteenth century brought a sea change to the Nickerson family, and likewise to the entire nation, as cities swelled from

Vesta (Walter Nickerson's oldest sister) and her husband, Clarence Gifford, sitting on the porch. *Ancestry.com.*

increased industry and immigration. In Woods Hole, this was a pivotal time, with the establishment of the Marine Biological Laboratory in 1888, the Pacific Guano Company going belly-up in 1889 and the initial development of Penzance Point in 1892.

Throughout the country, the rise of industrialization saw a growing gap between the living conditions of the "haves" and the "have-nots," compounded by a financial crisis in 1892. In the big cities, the newly arrived immigrants who worked in the factories suffered overcrowded living and perilous working conditions. Immigrants working in the fertilizer factory in Woods Hole had it better than most, with less crowding and cleansing breezes, but the wealth gap was overwhelming.

Enter the progressives. Progressive reformers believed the federal government was an ideal tool to keep corporate abuses in check. Like Joseph Story Fay, who sought to improve Woods Hole, the progressives felt empowered to improve society through action, both political and civic. The focus of the reformers was varied and covered slum conditions, labor exploitation, alcohol prohibition and women's suffrage. Often overlooked is the divisive nature of some of the progressive actions, which at times produced negative results. For example, reforming labor laws and the push for women's suffrage positively improved the lives of millions of people. However, the progressive effort to clean up slums and brothels, a major focus of temperance proponents, also resulted in discriminatory housing practices that lasted well into the twentieth century. The movement also fueled a growing interest in eugenics, bundled into the effort to "plan social development using expert knowledge in both the social and natural science."[66] A critical component for fixing societal ills, the progressives argued, was approaching the problems from a scientific standpoint, using advancements in medicine and engineering to solve these issues, an approach that did not always make allowances for human nature.

Woods Hole proved to be an ideal petri dish for this kind of vision. By 1890, the village was filled to the gills with scientists and young progressives. The prevalence of modern thinking was reflected in the interests and choices of many in the Nickerson family, and particularly the Nickerson daughters. For example, though her day-to-day life was fairly traditional, by joining the Woman's Christian Temperance Union, Vesta illustrated her independent, activist bona fides. At age twenty, the unmarried Minnie was supporting herself and living as a boarder several miles from her parents, as was her sister Clara. Another sister, Nettie, embraced the opportunities made possible by reformed property rights for women as she set her own course.

Illustrating what modern women could accomplish, youngest sister Florence partnered with her brother Arthur to open an ice cream shop in 1896 on Main Street (now Water Street) in Woods Hole. By then, the economy of the village was driven by three core industries: the scientific community, maritime commerce and servicing the needs of summer visitors. Few of the jobs within the science community were held by locals, so Arthur and Florence focused on the tourist trade. Arthur previously ran a shop at the far end of Main Street, and in 1896, he sold the business and opened his ice cream shop at the corner of Main and Railroad (now Luscombe) Streets, close to where summer visitors transited from the train to the ferry. Today this spot is home to Coffee Obsession, an iconic hangout for the scientific crowd and visitors alike.

Arthur picked an ideal location to exploit the tourist trade, just steps away from the ferry dock. He also was an early adopter of the

A.C. Nickerson's ice cream shop, 1895. It closed by 1900. Coffee Obsession now occupies that spot. *WHHM.*

Mrs. Snow's Dry Goods Store on Main (Water) Street, 1895. *WHHM.*

"Shop Local" concept, looking to attract nearby Falmouth residents who otherwise might shop in Boston or New Bedford. The newspaper reported that "Mr. Arthur Nickerson has opened his ice cream parlor on Main Street, the interior of the parlor is very nicely decorated. Mr. Nickerson has the finest fountain in the village. Miss Florence Nickerson is in attendance and all will receive a warm welcome and be waited on with kindness. Give him a call and be happy, leave your money in the town and you will help all the trades, don't go to New Bedford but give it to the merchants here who will treat you well."[67]

By all accounts, Florence was in charge of the shop, which operated only during the summer months, for soon after establishing the business, Arthur relocated to Stoneham, near Boston, where he found year-round work in a shoe shop. While it was not entirely unheard of for women to run retail operations, such as Mrs. Snow's Dry Goods, also on Woods Hole's Main Street, it was unusual for such businesses to be run by young, unmarried women, such as Florence.

Sadly, A.C. Nickerson's store did not survive long. After four years working in Stoneham, Arthur returned to the village, sold off his shop fixtures and stock and for the next few years worked a variety of jobs as a carpenter and boatman. Like so many in Woods Hole, Arthur adapted as the commercial needs of the village changed, never landing on Easy Street but managing to make a living. On occasion, he also helped out with his brother Walter's mail route to Tarpaulin Cove, and this led to tragedy.

On September 5, 1906, Arthur and his friend Wallace E. Young were heading back from Naushon Island after delivering the mail. They "were off Jobs Neck on the return trip when Nickerson undertook to show Young what a stiff boat he had. He climbed up in the small jiggermast aft, and as this seemed to make no impression on the craft he clambered up the larger mast forward, and out on the sprit, leaving Young at the tiller. A sudden puff of wind came along at this time, catching Young unawares, so that with the added weight at her masthead the little boat was capsized, both men being thrown into the water."[68]

After thirty minutes clinging to the mast with no rescuer in sight, the two men became chilled and set out for shore, about a mile away. They were spotted by a passing catboat, but in a scene right out of *Titanic*, Arthur began to tire and was unable to grasp the rope tossed to him, and he "sank out of sight."[69] His companion barely survived the ordeal. A powerful tide was running out when Arthur drowned, and his body was not recovered until September 16, washed up at Cuttyhunk, the southernmost island in the Elizabeth Island chain. Following his funeral, held at the Nobska Lighthouse, he was buried in the Woods Hole Cemetery, where his grave is marked with a rather grand but sadly misspelled tombstone. A-U-R-T-H-U-R. One wonders if there is a good story behind that error.

Gravestone of Arthur Nickerson in the Woods Hole Cemetery. He drowned in Vineyard Sound in 1906. But why is his name misspelled, AURTHUR? *Sheehy Collection.*

Walter, the middle child of the Nickerson clan, was flanked on either side by rather unconventional sisters, Nettie and Clara. His older sister Nettie was the first in the family to marry an "outsider," paving the way for her younger siblings, all of whom either married outsiders or not at all. She married her first husband, William G. Weir, an Irish-born coachman, in 1889 and they settled in Boston. A daughter, Elizabeth Moreland Weir, was born the following year, and eighteen months later, Nettie gave birth to twin boys in Falmouth. Nettie's joy was short-lived though, as baby Donald had a weak heart and died two months later, followed just three weeks later by the death of baby Roger from cholera infantum, an acute gastrointestinal illness that struck many infants in the late nineteenth century.[70]

The Weir-Nickerson marriage, perhaps irrevocably broken by the death of the twins, ended in separation and divorce, another first in the family. In 1896, Nettie married Edward Norton Bunker of Edgartown, Martha's Vineyard, a more traditional choice, as her second husband was descended of established seagoing Yankees. The couple lived in Washington, D.C., where Edward worked as a printer for the Government Printing Office, and they adopted a daughter, Gladys, in 1898. For the next twenty-five years, Washington, D.C., served as a satellite headquarters for the Nickersons, as Nettie's nephew, daughter, and sister would live there at various times.

While Nettie was settling into married life in the District of Columbia, her young daughter Elizabeth Weir was becoming a creature of Woods Hole. From an early age, Elizabeth spent summers with her grandparents at Nobska Point. Nettie's youngest sister, Florence, was her constant companion, and the two regularly traveled by train between Woods Hole and the nation's capital. As she grew older, Elizabeth spent much of the year in Woods Hole, attending the local school, and conversely, Florence started spending winters in Washington, D.C., with Nettie. It was not an unusual arrangement in those days for children to be placed in the care of relatives after a marriage fell apart.

Adjacent to the U.S. Capitol building in Washington, D.C., lies the lush and peaceful West Senate Park. Today, it serves as a buffer between the heavy traffic around Union Station and the serene Capitol grounds. In 1900, when Nettie and her husband lived here, the area bustled with activity. A row of townhouses, an eclectic assortment of styles and rooflines, ran up North Capitol Street from Constitution Avenue at the Capitol's northern edge. By 1913, the entire area had been razed. With the federal government growing as rapidly as the U.S. population, the architect of the Capitol expanded the green space around the Capitol grounds, bulldozing the residential buildings for several blocks.

If you visit the area today, you will find a large plaque dedicated to the spot where George Washington built two brick townhouses in 1798. The dwellings were remodeled several times, and as North Capitol Street was improved and graded quite severely over the next hundred years, lowering

Looking down North Capitol Street toward the Capitol dome in Washington, D.C., 1901. Nettie's townhouse can be seen in the distance at the far left. *Library of Congress.*

This rendering approximates the view of Union Station from Nettie's house at 232 North Capitol Street. *Library of Congress.*

the level of the road, two stories were added *under* George Washington's original structure, taking it from three to five stories.[71]

A few doors down from this building stood 232 North Capitol Street, the residence of Nettie, Edward and Gladys Bunker. Edward worked at the enormous U.S. Government Printing Office that still stands at 732 North Capitol Street, while Nettie ran a private maternity hospital at 139 Massachusetts Avenue NE, just around the corner from her home. They lived in the literal heart of the city.

Nettie's presence in Washington, D.C., brought other family members to the area. After her brother's shop closed, Nettie's younger sister Florence began spending a significant part of the year with the Bunkers on Capitol Hill, and in 1904, their nephew Waldo Gifford also moved to town. Having completed his studies at Bryant & Stretton Commercial College in Boston, Waldo found work as a bookkeeper at Washington Brewery Company, located at Fourth and E Streets NE, which may not have sat well with his temperance-driven mother, Vesta, but it was a good, steady job. Breweries experienced tremendous growth during this period as waves of new immigrants from Germany, Ireland and Poland arrived. Across the country, beer's popularity exploded, with per capita annual consumption doubling, from twenty-eight gallons per person in 1890 to sixty gallons in 1910.[72] Little did Waldo know that breweries would be forced to close in

1919 with the establishment of the Volstead Act, prohibiting the production and sale of alcohol from 1920 to 1933.

On New Year's Eve 1909, Waldo married Kathryn Elizabeth Connelly, and they settled on Second Street NW, just a few blocks from his aunts Nettie and Florence. His cousin Gladys attended St. Cecelia's School, a Catholic girls' school just a few blocks from her home. Edward joined the Grand Lodge, Knights of the Pythias, a fraternal organization whose membership included William Jennings Bryan and Warren Harding and, later, Louis Armstrong. They all traveled frequently to spend time in Woods Hole, and the Bunkers appeared to live an exemplary life. Until it fell apart.

Under the headline "Tire of Married Life," the *Washington Post* reported that Nettie Bunker had filed suit for a separation from her husband, who she alleged "is given to excessive use of intoxicating liquors."[73] The suit alleged that Edward had deserted her, and she requested alimony and custody of Gladys. Though the Bunkers were not high society in Washington, D.C., this was newsworthy in July 1908. The divorce proceedings dragged out into the following year and were carefully detailed by both the *Washington Post* and the *Washington Evening Star.*

In early 1909, Nettie feared Edward would leave the District of Columbia to avoid his financial responsibilities. He was arrested on a *writ of ne exeat* (essentially an order not to leave the jurisdiction), but the judge found no cause and he was released. When her separation request was denied in May, Nettie filed another suit the following day. "Declaring that she had been left destitute by the alleged desertion of her husband, Nettie M. Bunker yesterday filed suit for maintenance in the District Supreme Court against Edward N. Bunker."[74] Nettie was relentless in pushing for justice, and in December, she was finally granted her divorce, along with "twenty-five dollars per month allowed as alimony, in addition to an allowance of $50 for counsel fees."[75]

Nettie had held strong and prevailed in court. Six months later, Edward was again arrested and indicted by a grand jury for "non-support of wife and child." Nettie had been right about him after all.

Divorce, though becoming more common, carried a social stigma and presented economic challenges in 1910. About one in sixteen marriages ended in divorce, and Nettie had two divorces to her name. Though property laws had changed by then to allow married women to keep their wages and property, they remained in a fragile position. For whatever reason, social or financial, starting in 1911 Nettie listed herself in the local directory as a widow, though Edward remained very much alive. He moved back to Boston and in 1922 married Sabina F. Bradley, a childhood friend. He died in Boston in 1929 and is buried in Edgartown.

Nettie had only just emerged from her messy divorce when she became embroiled in another legal saga, one that might have ruined a lesser woman. As reported in the *Washington Post*, "Mrs. R.L. Frazier, who conducts a maternity hospital at 139 Massachusetts avenue northeast…was arrested yesterday in connection with the crusade against alleged misuse of the mails."[76] Mrs. Frazier was the pseudonym Nettie Bunker used in her professional work. She pleaded not guilty to the charge.

Nettie's arrest was part of a nationwide dragnet conducted by the Division of Inspection of the Post Office Department, which made 142 arrests across the country in a single day, in an effort to crack down on the practice of abortion. In the nineteenth century, abortion laws varied throughout the country and were difficult to prosecute, but by 1910, abortion had been made illegal in all fifty states. Sting operations such as this were intended to give teeth to the law.

That same day, another D.C. resident, Dr. Thomas J. Kemp, was also arrested in the sweep, but most of the newspaper ink was reserved for "Mrs. Frazier," despite—or perhaps because of—him being the son-in-law of Senator Fletcher, the longest-serving senator in Florida's history. Dr. Kemp's wedding, just seven months prior to his arrest, was attended by congressmen, cabinet members and even President Taft.

Nettie "made no objection to her arrest…denied that there was any basis for the charge against her, and said she was confident of being acquitted."[77] Specifically, she was accused of responding to a decoy letter mailed from North Carolina seeking information on abortion services. She "freely admitted that she conducts a maternity hospital and that she advertises in the newspapers. But she denied that she had sent any obscene literature or anything relating to illegal practices through the mails."[78]

Nettie and Dr. Kemp were indicted by a grand jury, "charged with violating section 211 of the United States penal code by sending improper matter through the mails."[79] By all accounts, Nettie comported herself with confidence and dignity throughout the trial. She stuck to her "unalterable statement" that "while she wrote the decoy answer for the purpose of misleading the writer of what was the decoy letter, she did so only for the purpose of getting the prospective patient into her hands, with the hope that the patient could be persuaded to remain for a stipulated time at her Massachusetts avenue house, for which a fee of $300 was to be charged. She flatly denied that she wrote the letter to accomplish the purpose charged by the government."[80]

On March 28, Nettie M. Bunker was found not guilty. For the second time in five years, Nettie held her ground in court, and again she prevailed. Dr. Kemp was less fortunate at convincing the jury of his innocence, as two days earlier he was found guilty and sentenced to two years in the penitentiary, along with a $500 fine. Immediately following Nettie's acquittal, Dr. Kemp's attorney appealed his conviction, and though he ultimately lost in court, his sentence was commuted the following year, such that he merely had to pay the $500 fine, about $15,000 today. "The commutation, from the Department of Justice bore the great red seal of the United States and the signature of the president."[81] House Minority Leader, Republican James Robert Mann, cried foul that President Wilson would reward a fellow Democrat's son-in-law in this manner, but his protests came to naught.

In contrast to her adventurous sister, Walter's younger sister Clara lived a more traditional life, at least from outward appearances. In 1900, with Nettie and Florence living in Washington, D.C., Clara was living on Main Street in downtown Falmouth, listed on the U.S. Census as a boarder in the household of Ernest P. Nutter. Ernest was a confectioner in the seaside town, and on the 1900 census, he claimed to be a widower. A year later, Clara and Ernest were married, making the recent living arrangement—in a small town, no less—rather scandalous. It is unclear whether Clara knew her husband's marital history at the time of the wedding, but one suspects she figured it out eventually.

In truth, Ernest *had* been widowed in 1890, when his twenty-three-year-old bride, Effie Kennedy, died during childbirth in Boston. However, he was no grieving widower when Clara was his boarder in Falmouth. Six months after Effie's death, Ernest married Helen "Nellie" Atwood, who gave birth to their daughter, Ruth Plumer Nutter, seven months after the wedding. What happened next is unclear, but it did not end well for Nellie and Ruth.

While Ernest was living in Falmouth selling confections to the summer people, the census shows that Nellie and Ruth Nutter were living in Dorchester, a divorced woman and her eight-year-old daughter. By 1910, eighteen-year-old Ruth lived in a Boston boardinghouse not far from her mother, in a rundown neighborhood near the City Jail. She was an unemployed nurse and her mother was a hospital cook. A year later, the unmarried Ruth Nutter died at Boston Lying-In Hospital from eclampsia, a rare complication during pregnancy more common in young first-time mothers, especially if poor nutrition is an issue.

In a fascinating twist, Ruth Nutter, seemingly abandoned by her father as a child, was buried in the Nutter family plot in Lindenwood Cemetery, Stoneham, Massachusetts. Her simple (but quite large) stone sits adjacent to her paternal grandparents and great-grandparents (Plumers and Nutters), and she would eventually be joined by her father in 1931, whose complicated final years meant that he was not buried near Clara. And

Ruth Nutter's prominent gravestone sits in the foreground, with her mother buried two rows back (*left*) at Lindenwood Cemetery in Stoneham, Massachusetts. Ruth's estranged father lies in an unmarked grave near her feet. *Sheehy Collection.*

remarkably, just a few feet away in the same cemetery, sits the headstone of her mother, Nellie. In 1916, Nellie married George Wyman, a widower, and when Nellie died in 1934, George (who intended to be buried with his first wife) purchased a family plot in the same section of the Lindenwood Cemetery where Ruth is buried. Several of the Wyman children are buried alongside their stepmother, and the Nutter family, estranged in life, was together in the end.[82]

As for Clara, she and her husband moved to Salem, Massachusetts, in 1907 when Ernest shifted his career from shopkeeper to shoemaker, and on the surface, her life seemed calm. Though they had no children of their own, Clara took a deep interest in the welfare of her nieces Elizabeth and Gladys and remained in close contact with her sisters throughout. She eventually returned to Cape Cod but, for many years, was content to serve as an outpost for relatives, and her connection to the Nickerson family and Woods Hole remained strong.

## 9

# WALTER NICKERSON AT THE HELM

W hile his siblings were wandering the Eastern Seaboard, Walter was content to remain in Woods Hole. Walter Eugene Nickerson was born in Chatham on September 5, 1867, the fifth child and second son of Oliver Arey and Mary Elizabeth Nickerson. After leaving school at thirteen, he earned a living from the sea as a boatman, lobsterman and mailman. Walter learned to sail when he was young, and he knew every inch of water surrounding Woods Hole and the Naushon Islands. He fished and kept lobster traps, and in the winter, Walter cut ice from the local ponds to be used, or sold off, during the warmer months.

Walter's primary occupation was contracting as a government mail carrier, with responsibility for running the route to Tarpaulin Cove on Naushon Island, just offshore of Woods Hole. It was a stable job with good pay, bringing him $525 annually.[83] In the precarious world of boatmen, this was reliable income. He would pick up the post from the morning train at the Woods Hole depot and deliver it by boat to the tiny post office on Naushon Island; then he would carry mail from the island back to Woods Hole. Over the years, Walter developed several entrepreneurial strategies to combine his various occupations. As relayed in an interview with a Woods Hole local, Oscar Hilton, Walter would meet the train and "take the mailbag. He used to have lobster pots on the Sound. He'd carry the mail up, and he'd haul the traps when the tide showed right so he could get them. Then, he figured he'd go to the Cove with the mail and then get the mailbag back again."[84]

The Ship Store and Post Office at Tarpaulin Cove on Naushon Island. *WHHM.*

Walter Nickerson's career as a contracted mail carrier ended in 1916 once the "post office at Tarpaulin cove [had] been discontinued. In the last year of its existence, it took about $800 to pay the messenger to carry the mail to and from Woods Hole while the receipts of the office were about $13."[85] Even the Forbes family, owners of the private island, couldn't justify the lopsided financials.

Lobstering, one of his side jobs, proved quite lucrative, and at the time of his death Walter owned two lobster boats and eighty lobster traps, many stacked up along the seawall behind the house.[86] In 1894, the *Falmouth Enterprise* reported that "according to a report of Isaiah Young, commissioner of inland fisheries and game, for the year ending December 31, 1893 [the quantity of] marketable lobster were taken in this town as follows: Woods Holl [as it was spelled from 1877 to 1896]…191 traps 7428 lobsters."[87] Walter Nickerson, along with his older brother, Alfred, was one of fourteen lobstermen who took in that haul. With a market rate of eighteen to twenty cents per pound in 1894, that was a nice chunk of change.

Walter discovered that the warmer months presented additional opportunities for income. Woods Hole attracted an increasing number of "summer people," including scientists who spent the summer collecting and studying specimens from the local waters. Walter earned extra money taking these visitors out in his boat while subcontracting his mail services with some of the local boatmen. Prince Crowell, grandson of the founder of the Pacific

Guano Company, was a terrific sailor. Born in Woods Hole in 1881, Prince honed his boat skills in Vineyard Sound and learned some special tricks thanks to Walter Nickerson's mail route. In an interview with the *Yarmouth Register*, he shared that "the man who had the mail contract found it more profitable to take charter parties so I sailed the mail for him. I'd stop at the ship store on Naushon and they'd have a bowl of milk and crackers ready for my lunch." Later, he mentioned that he learned how to ride the wakes of other boats on the sound and successfully used this trick to his advantage in sailing competitions.[88]

This is not to say that Walter Nickerson did not take his job seriously. He prided himself on rarely missing a mail delivery. In 1911, he was forced to take a day off due to high winds, for which Woods Hole is famous. "Walter Nickerson, mail carrier to Tarpaulin Cove, who has not missed a trip this winter, did not undertake to convey mail there Thursday on account of the furious westerly gale. Mr. Nickerson uses a power catboat to make the six-mile trip up the sound."[89] Those who know the strong winds that inhabit Woods Hole in the winter—well, year-round, truth be told—can appreciate Walter's dedication.

Sometimes Walter would find flotsam during his rounds, such as the bales of hay he reported seeing in the sound in 1900, or the items he posted in the newspaper's lost items section: "Found in Vineyard Sound: August 1, 13-foot rowboat which the owner can have by proving property and paying charges. Apply to W.E. Nickerson, Woods Hole."[90] He also collected "gasoline, engine, gaff and boom" during his one of his rounds.

One of Walter E. Nickerson's discoveries was quite distressing, as reported in the newspaper in April 1906.

> *The body of Captain Washington Robbins of Cotuit, for many years master of the schooner* Mary B Wellington, *was found on the shore of Lackeys cove, Naushon, Monday by Walter Nickerson.*
>
> *Mr. Nickerson, who discovered the body, is mail carrier to Naushon, and he saw the body on the beach when he left on the arrival of the 10.08 train at Woods Hole. As he did not want to go to the body alone, he returned to Woods Hole, and with Captain Charles Grinnell in the latter's motor boat, they went together to Lackey's cove.*[91]

Only five months later, Walter's own brother Arthur would suffer a similar fate in the same area. Even for experienced sailors, the currents that run through the hole with every tide can be deadly. In January 1912, the

*Falmouth Enterprise* reported that a "mast of the schooner that was wrecked near Cuttyhunk [the outermost of the Elizabeth Islands] recently was towed into Little Harbor on Wed by Captain Walter Nickerson."[92]

Here, finally, our hero is referred to as "Captain"!

Research made it clear that Walter Nickerson was never a sea captain and that he had not traveled to China as Mary Ramsbottom had been told. Still, he was given the title of captain on a number of occasions. It was a sure sign of respect that his father, Oliver Nickerson, was addressed as Captain Nickerson in his 1911 obituary, though he had not commanded a vessel for forty years or more. Over the years, Walter must have similarly earned the respect of his fellow sailors for his unparalleled boating skills, earning him the title of Captain Walter Nickerson from his peers.

Indeed, Walter Nickerson was a skilled sailor, mastering the small craft particular to the area, and he managed to pocket significant prize money in the competitive races off Woods Hole. In the late nineteenth century, Woods Hole racing was dominated by catboats, spritsails and knockabouts, small and sturdy sailing craft particularly well-suited to the region. For many years, the boats entered in local races were the working craft of fishermen who made a living on the waters around Woods Hole, and they were heavy and cumbersome. The Woods Hole Open Town Regatta was established in 1884, when Walter was seventeen years old, and so began a change in the sailing vessels that raced on Vineyard Sound. While there were still some working catboats and spritsails in that regatta, owned both by local mariners and summer residents, the move was already shifting to modern racing boats, designed for speed, unlike the clunkier traditional fishing boats.

The divide between working boats and racing craft illustrates one aspect of the tension between the locals and the "outsiders." Local bias is evident in the editorial comments of an 1897 news article in the *Falmouth Enterprise*: "Two catboats, *Never Touch Me* and *Clio*, both of New Bedford, have been pulled from the ledge in Woods Hole, having become lodged there through the ignorance of their skippers. The rescue work is being done by Capt. J.J. Veeder in the launch *Dagetta*."[93] The writer did not suffer fools (or city folk) gladly.

Interest in racing increased with the establishment of the Woods Hole Yacht Club in 1896, and with it came generous prize money, often provided by wealthy summer members. A.C. Harrison of Philadelphia, who owned a home on Little Harbor, was an enthusiastic patron of the local races and offered up lavish lunches in his boathouse between races. Walter took advantage of the opportunity to monetize his outstanding

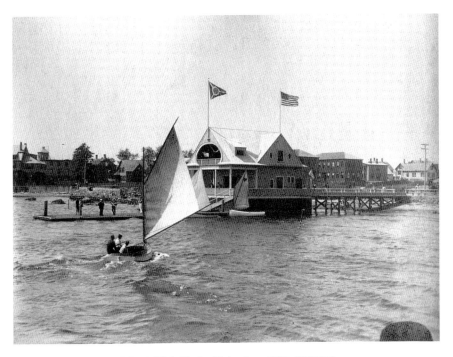

Catboat at the original Woods Hole Yacht Club, circa 1900. *WHHM.*

seamanship. On July 4, 1897, the boat races were the highlight of the holiday weekend.

*The Fourth passed off very quietly in this place. No serious accidents being reported up to date. The only excitement of the day was two boat races off Penzance in the afternoon. Mr. S. Cahoon in his own boat,* The Politician, *succeeded in winning first prize in the special race, and Mr. Walter E. Nickerson, in a boat built and owned by Norton & Grinnell, was awarded the prize in the second race sailed. The sea was very smooth and the wind very light, and the time made was very slow. Large crowds gathered at different places along the course, and considerable excitement prevailed at the finish of both races as the difference in time between the first and second boats was very slight.*[94]

Walter's secret weapon was his unparalleled knowledge of the currents and his mastery of capturing even the slightest bit of wind to move his vessel along. In September 1899, Walter managed a fifth-place finish, with prize money attached, against fourteen Class B Spritsail boats that were raced by some of the better-known sailors in Woods Hole. He had a big win in 1901 as well, earning twenty-five dollars for two hours, forty-one minutes and thirty-six seconds' work. Once again, the reporter makes clear his bias toward the local working sailor:

> *The catboat race for prizes offered by A.C. Harrison of Woods Hole, one of the most enthusiastic yachtsmen on the Cape, was sailed Friday afternoon of last week off Little harbor, in a single reef breeze from the southwest.*
>
> *The course selected was up the sound to Tarpaulin cove, thence to Lucas shoals and return, a distance of 15 miles, five of which gave the skippers good windward work.*
>
> *The prizes were $25, $20, $15, $12, $10, $8, $6, and $4, and the first was captured by the* **Nobska**, *sailed by Walter Nickerson, who handled his boat very cleverly, defeating* **Mollie**, *the second boat, by more than three minutes. Skipper Nickerson's knowledge of the Vineyard sound tides helped him considerably, and enabled him to get a splendid lead which the others were unable to overcome.*[95]

In 1905, Walter Nickerson took third place in the IOU race off Little Harbor, with Franklin L. Gifford serving as judge of the boat race. In 1906, the *Trilby*, owned by Mr. Perdum and sailed by Captain Walter Nickerson took, second in a July race. His fourth-place finish in the *Nobska* in September 1906 earned him ten dollars. It would appear Walter retired from boat racing shortly thereafter.[96]

Whether it was age, health or his new role of husband that put an end to Walter's racing, there was rising tension within the local racing community and Walter likely felt it. As John Valois noted in his piece "Woods Hole Yacht Club: Early Years" in *Woods Hole Reflections*, "Two major causes of dissatisfaction were the modern designed spritsails and the dues paid by fishermen. The racing spritsails were built light and fast....Heavy boats could not match the speeds of the lighter ones. This led to discouragement among those who could not compete. The dues of the working fishermen were set at a reduced rate. A number of the fishermen were winning the cash prizes and spending considerable sums to maintain 'racing trim.' This conflict of ethics did not seem correct to some members."[97] Walter likely irked some of the racing crowd by winning so many cash prizes, especially as he was simultaneously paying lower dues, but he wasn't spending his money on "racing trim." He was investing in real estate.

By 1901, Walter had saved enough money to purchase property in Crow Hill, which sits atop the land overlooking Eel Pond. He purchased a lot on Middle Street from his sister Vesta and her husband, Clarence Gifford, for $550. The Giffords lived on High Street, across from the corner lot, empty nesters, as their only child, Waldo, was studying in Boston at the time. This would be Walter's home until 1917, when he moved to Millfield Street, at which point he rented it out, earning him additional income during the summer months and occasionally even during the off-season.

*10*

# THE DAWN OF A NEW CENTURY

As the country entered the twentieth century, chaos was everywhere. The United States was on war footing in the Pacific and Cuba; President McKinley was assassinated by an anarchist, putting Theodore Roosevelt into the White House; and modern conveniences like electricity were reaching the lower classes. Labor strikes in the 1890s resulted in better working conditions for most, including a shorter workday. The extra leisure time was filled with various pleasures, including circuses and sport. Baseball was already the national pastime, and it competed for attention with basketball, introduced in Springfield, Massachusetts, in 1891, while football primarily remained a college sport. The first decade of the new century would prove to be tumultuous for the Nickerson family. It would bring three weddings, two divorces, two healthy babies, one infant death and one fatal accident.

The decade started well enough. Vesta, Nettie and Clara had settled into married life. The rest of the Nickerson clan went about their various occupations, weaving in and out of the village for holidays and to spend time with family. By 1900, only Florence and Herman, the baby of the family, remained at home, though official documents tell a different story.

In 1903, at the age of thirty-six, Walter got married, and like Nettie and Clara, he married an outsider. As he did not travel much, he likely met his future bride in Falmouth, which was a holiday destination for people from all over New England. Helena C. Nugent was a twenty-eight-year-old schoolteacher from Clinton, Massachusetts, near Worcester, and may have visited the Cape during a school break. It was an unconventional pairing, as she was the daughter of an Irish immigrant marrying an establishment New Englander. And she was Roman Catholic.

Imagine the drama surrounding this event. Walter and Helena were married on October 28, 1903, at St. John the Evangelist Catholic Church in Clinton, where she grew up. Walter's youngest brother, Herman, was an official witness, and presumably the Nugent clan was there in full force. The ceremony was performed by Father John J. O'Keefe, the pastor of St. John's, who was also, due to the close relationship between Father O'Keefe and the Nugent family, the employer of Helena's sister, Gertrude.

The Nickerson ancestors had come to America in 1637 in search of economic opportunity and religious freedom. They were Puritan Congregationalists who had fled Catholic repression in Europe and over eight generations had established themselves as the bedrock of Massachusetts society. Oliver Nickerson, Walter's father, was a dedicated member of the Church of the Messiah, the oldest Episcopal church on Cape Cod. Church of the Messiah is a visible and ecumenical focal point of the village, with the Woods Hole Cemetery adjacent, where most of Woods Hole's early citizens of diverse faiths are buried.

By contrast, Helena was a first-generation American from a devout Roman Catholic family. Like the Nickersons, the Nugents came to America in search of economic opportunity and religious freedom. When Helena's father, Felix Nugent, arrived in New York from Belfast in 1845, the Catholic population in New England was beginning to explode, as Irish, Italian and German immigrants arrived in search of work and economic self-reliance. The church was the center of daily life, so Catholics tended to settle in groups close to the local church, and it was unusual to marry outside the faith. Though how Walter and Helena met and the circumstances under which they courted remain unclear, the Nickerson and Nugent families became closely entwined in each other's lives, despite the religious divide.

Walter and Helena settled into the house on Middle Street. Details of the goings-on of Mr. and Mrs. Walter E. Nickerson come mostly from the archives of the *Falmouth Enterprise*. Throughout much of the early twentieth century, residents of Falmouth could scarcely make a move without it being accounted for in the weekly paper. This must have been stifling at times for the subjects of the news items, but one hundred years, later it is a researcher's gold mine.

The earliest mention of Helena in the paper was in 1905, when it is reported that "whooping cough descended on Woods Hole" and that Mrs.

Walter Nickerson, along with her sister-in-law and niece, was "among the inflicted."[98] By 1908, visits of her sister Gertrude and niece Grace appeared regularly in the Woods Hole section of the paper.

The year 1909 was an eventful one for Walter and Helena. In March, Helena gave birth to Joseph Nugent Nickerson in Clinton, where she grew up. Sadly, her mother died just a few months later, and when Grace and her brother James came to Woods Hole for a visit in November, Grace stayed on and spent the winter helping her aunt. Over the next few decades, Woods Hole would hold a special place in Grace's life, while Clinton connections became increasingly important in the future of Walter and Helena.

BEFORE SHIFTING THE FOCUS to Clinton, Massachusetts, there are two other Nickerson family members to mention. Walter's oldest and youngest brothers, Alfred and Herman, were born seventeen years apart, and their lives were equally disparate. Like Walter, Alfred was a skilled boatman, and though he briefly left the village for work when he was a young man, he soon returned and never left again. Alfred had a short stint with the Pilots' Association in Boston, returning to serve as the pilot tender off Nobska Point for the next fifty years, helping vessels as they came through the challenging shoals around Woods Hole at all hours of the night and in all kinds of weather.

The role of pilot tender was critical to the shipping lanes along the New England coast. Due to the treacherous nature of the waters off the Cape, ships employed pilots, experts in navigating the tricky coastline, who would board vessels in Boston and then guide them past the shallow waters at the mouth of Vineyard Sound. The pilot tender and his small boat would meet up with vessels at a scheduled time and transport the pilot back to shore, so he could return to Boston by train and pilot the next boat.

Alfred was renowned for his reliability, and the one time he was late meeting a pilot, it made the newspaper. It was in March 1938, and Alfred was seventy-five years old. Eight paragraphs were devoted to the story of the large ship helplessly floating offshore, awaiting the arrival of the pilot tender. It was big news in the village, since the loud pleading horn blasts coming from the stranded ship at midnight woke up most of Woods Hole. Apparently, Alfred's assistant had fallen asleep in his car and hadn't shown up to help prepare the boat. Alfred explained that the poor lad "didn't wake up until he heard the ship's horn. But I don't blame Bob. I'll take all the responsibility myself. Guess once in 50 years isn't so bad."[99] Of course,

Alfred Nickerson, relaxing at home. *WHHM.*

this story became part of Woods Hole lore and found its way into Alfred's obituary five years later.

In addition to his pilot tender duties, Alfred was a longtime employee of the Falmouth Highway Department, responsible for maintaining the Woods Hole streets. Like so many residents of Woods Hole, Alfred cobbled together a number of jobs to ensure his financial survival. In doing so, he successfully straddled the transition from the dominance of ship traffic in the nineteenth century to the emergence of automobile traffic in the twentieth century, adapting his skills for the changing times. He was a reliable and respected member of the Woods Hole community.

And then there was Herman Nickerson, the baby—and black sheep—of the Nickerson clan. Herman was born in the newly built keeper's house at Nobska Point around 1878 (his birth certificate remains elusive), so leaking roofs and overcrowded bedrooms did not feature into his childhood. He was able to stay in school until he was seventeen and spent some time away from Woods Hole after graduating. Upon his return to the village, Herman developed a business as a "poultry raiser," first at Nobska and later

LIFE AND HISTORY ON EEL POND

on Quissett Avenue, and expanded into selling eggs for hatching, as well as owning milk cows. He advertised his eggs in the *Falmouth Enterprise* with the rather exclusive mailing address of "Box 3" at the Woods Hole Post Office. In his early twenties, he had all the makings of a successful entrepreneur.

Alas, his road to success was short-lived. In 1905, at age twenty-six he married Agda Helena Melby, a Swedish immigrant. It really shouldn't have surprised Herman that his new wife was strong and independent. She had to rely on herself and her sharp wit from a young age, traveling alone to America at age seventeen. After returning briefly to Sweden, she came back to New York in 1903 when she was twenty-five. The couple wed in Manhattan and moved to Woods Hole.

In 1907, Agda gave birth to a daughter, naming her Helena Florence Nickerson. Just four days later, the baby died suddenly, her death certificate indicating a weak heart. The couple seemed to recover, joining village activities like Saturday Night Whist Club games and various entertainments offered at Liberty Hall in the months that followed.

But things were clearly not well in the Herman Nickerson household. In November 1908, just a few months after Nettie filed for divorce from Edward Bunker, Agda left Woods Hole for New York, staying with her sister's family in Peekskill, fifty miles north of New York City. By December 1909, Herman had sold his dairy business and headed to New York himself, planning to "engage in the restaurant business."[100] After spending the winter in New York, he returned to Woods Hole in March 1910, alone.

One month later, on April 5 in Peekskill, Agda gave birth to a baby boy, whom she named Carl Melby Nickerson. There is nothing to indicate that Herman was involved in Carl's life, though he did return to New York in 1911, possibly focused on reconciling with his wife. However, the newspaper reported that he was back in Woods Hole after a short time away, so if that was his game plan, it failed. Agda maintained her married status officially for a time, indicating she was "widowed" on the 1920 census and then "divorced" by 1930. Carl remained in Peekskill for the rest of his life, running a restaurant for many years and then an antique shop, but he and his wife, Greta, had no children.

After Agda left him, Herman's life spiraled further out of control. He returned to his childhood home, living at Nobska Point with his parents and Florence, who was helping her father, tracking passing vessels for his official keeper's log. Next door in the smaller building lived the assistant keeper, George Cameron. George and his wife, Edith Snow Cameron, had arrived in Falmouth in 1910 from Baker's Island Light Station in Salem Harbor, where George had been the assistant keeper since 1905. They brought with them three children, and in April 1910, one day after Carl Nickerson was born in Peekskill, Edith gave birth to twin boys in Falmouth.[101]

When Oliver Nickerson died in June 1911, George Cameron was promoted to head lightkeeper, moving his family into the main house. Oliver's widow and daughter moved to School Street, but George allowed Herman to stay on as a boarder, which proved an unfortunate decision.

George had his hands full running the lighthouse complex, especially as Florence was no longer logging the heavy ship traffic. Though it was not his fault in the least, when the Boston-bound steamer *Bunker Hill* ran aground off Nobska Point in August of that first year, George's world started to fray. In October, Edith reportedly "took their children and ran off to parts unknown with Herman."[102]

The coupling of Edith and Herman was short-lived. By 1913, George Cameron had given up his post at Nobska and returned to the Salem area, reconciling with Edith and settling in Lynn. Sadly, Edith suffered from chronic endocarditis, and just two years later, she died of a cerebral embolism, brought on by her poor health and further complicated by pregnancy. She gave birth to a son the day she died. Overwhelmed, George gave the baby up for adoption.

And what about the black sheep, Herman? After he and Edith parted ways, Herman left Massachusetts and headed west, eventually landing in Galveston, Texas, where he worked a variety of jobs, including janitor, law office clerk, painter and deliveryman. Herman died in Galveston in 1958, aged eighty-four, and is buried in Seabrook, Texas. He was the only child of Oliver and Mary Nickerson not to spend his later years in Woods Hole and only one of two not buried in the village cemetery (the other being Walter, a Catholic convert, who is buried in Clinton). His scandalous behavior, no doubt seared into the memories of Woods Hole residents, may have shamed him to sever permanently his ties to the village of his birth.

In October 1912, Helena Nickerson gave birth to a stillborn baby boy at the House of Mercy in Pittsfield, Massachusetts. The *Falmouth Enterprise* made note of her return to Woods Hole in November 1912,[103] yet it is unlikely that her neighbors were aware of the pregnancy before she left for Pittsfield in late spring, having rented out the house for the summer months.

Her sister Gertrude was living in Dalton, not far from Pittsfield, working as the housekeeper for Father John J. O'Keefe, now pastor at St. Agnes, and the priest who had celebrated Helena's marriage to Walter. Baby Nickerson was buried on October 14 at Fairview Cemetery, the final resting place for working-class Irish Catholics in Dalton. No doubt the seventy-year-old Father O'Keefe was a consoling figure for Helena in her grief, further strengthening the bond between them. And research reveals that without such a strong bond, the house on Millfield might never have come to be.

The next few years would be a major turning point in the lives of Walter, Helena and their son Joseph. Without also understanding the family history of the Nugents, it is difficult to understand how things came about. Like Woods Hole, both families were touched by economic challenges, tragedies and change, and they called upon the same adaptability, resilience and strength of relationship, prevalent throughout the village, to carry on.

# 11

# NUGENTS IN THE NEW WORLD

In 1903, the marriage of Walter Nickerson and Helena Nugent connected two families from very different worlds. The comparison of the Nickerson and Nugent families goes well beyond the Protestant-Catholic divide. The Nickersons arrived in America in the 1600s and became part of the establishment, while the Nugents arrived in the 1840s and belonged to the new immigrant class that populated the mill towns of the Northeast. For centuries, the Nickersons were people of the sea, just as the Nugents were farmers, tied to the land. Yet there are similarities in the way relationships bound together members in each of these large families, especially as the older generation looked out for the welfare of young children caught up in the tragedies of their parents' lives.

Unlike the Nickersons, there is no Nugent homestead in America, nor a large organization, such as the Nickerson Family Association in Chatham. The Nugent legacy includes farms, though the buildings are mostly gone, and the churches they helped build, many of which still welcome worshippers.

This is their story.

LIFE IN NINETEENTH-CENTURY IRELAND was not easy. Uprisings in 1798 were brutally put down by the British, but the push for emancipation of the Irish Catholics grew steadily, running headlong into the dual crises of poverty and starvation.

The oppressive system of landownership was a significant factor in both the severity of the Great Famine (1845–52) and the mindset of the Nugents who came to America. British landlords forced Irish peasants onto small plots of land that could barely sustain their large families. Potatoes, which required little labor and thrived in the meager soil, became an essential crop, but increased reliance of the population on a single staple was fraught with risk. When a devastating fungus arrived in 1845, withering the potato crops almost overnight, there was massive starvation across the island. During the ensuing years, out of a population of eight million people, over one million Irish died and another million immigrated to America, creating a different sort of famine in Ireland, a famine of able-bodied youth.

This is the backdrop of the immigrant story of the Francis Nugent family, so similar to the story of other Irish immigrants but with one important twist: the first Nugent came to America months before the blight appeared.

Francis, patriarch of the Nugent family, was a land steward in Ireland, managing the estate of a wealthy landowner. Compared to many, his life enjoyed some stability, but his opportunities were minimal. He lived in a stone cottage with a thatched roof and dirt floors and eked out a living on his small garden plot with no long-term security for the family of eight. He and his wife, Catherine "Margaret" Duffy, had five sons and one daughter.

Felix Nugent, Helena's father, was born in 1825, the third son of Francis and Margaret Nugent. The family lived in Monaghan, not far from where the Northern Ireland border would be set a century later. Beginning in the seventeenth century, there was ongoing conflict between Gaelic Catholics and the British Protestant community that formed around Ulster, only seventy miles north of Monaghan. It was in this climate of religious and cultural oppression that Felix Nugent grew up. During his childhood, the tension was rampant, forcing Felix to attend night schools, as the regular schools around Ulster were under Protestant control.

Unlike most Irish immigrant stories, it was political turmoil and land scarcity, not crop failure, that fueled Felix Nugent's desire to emigrate. He left Ireland in early 1845, months before the first potato plants showed signs of blight. Frustrated by the lack of opportunity despite working hard, Felix was motivated to leave Ireland after the death of his father. He saw an opportunity in the tragedy. Felix "worked with his father after leaving school, but, when his father died in 1844, he resolved to try his fortunes in a new

Irish emigrants leaving home—the priest's blessing, 1851. *New York Public Library.*

country where men could hold property in their own right, uncursed by the landlord system."[104]

Felix arrived in New York in April 1845, a twenty-year-old with no connections, and was soon followed by his brother John. The brothers worked in the city, and by 1850, the rest of his family, including his widowed mother, had made the difficult journey to America. By the time the potato blight peaked, forcing an exodus from Ireland, Felix had acclimated to his new country and knew where to look for opportunity. The entire family moved to West Boylston, Massachusetts, in 1850, working in the textile mills. Work in the mills drew hundreds of newly arrived Irish immigrants to the area, creating pockets of Irish culture amid the land of Yankees. Though Felix and his siblings came to America to farm, initially they were content with work that the factory provided, ensuring they could feed their families. At their core, though, the Nugents were farmers, and they came to America in search of land.

Felix's brother John was the first to ditch factory work, heading to Wilton, Illinois, with modest savings and his new bride, Eleanor "Ellen" McCarthy. Opportunity awaited in the Midwest, where the U.S. government was anxious to settle its recently acquired western lands, and landownership was attainable for hardworking farmers. With eighty acres under his control, unimaginable back in Ireland, John began farming.

One by one, three other Nugent brothers—Francis, Mathew and Michael—migrated to Wilton, securing their own land until, by the end of the Civil War, they collectively controlled 720 acres. Faith was central to their lives, and the Nugents helped build St. Patrick's Roman Catholic Church in the township, with John leading the first Lay Committee. The church was destroyed by a tornado almost as soon as it was completed, but the community held strong and rebuilt it. The church then burned down in 1897 and again in 1929. The wooden building finally was replaced with one made of brick, and it welcomes worshippers to this day.

Over the next decade, the Wilton Nugents had twenty-three children. Like their local church, a number of tragedies struck the family in those early years, starting when Francis died in 1854 at the age of thirty-one, leaving his wife, Maryann, alone with her young daughter. John Nugent was left a widower in 1867, but his daughter took over housekeeping duties and they carried on, unaware that the worst was yet to come.

In 1868, Mathew was returning from a trip to Joliette when his wagon got stuck in the road. The weather had suddenly turned cold and wet, and he died of exposure during the night.[105] His wife, Catherine, was pregnant with their seventh child, and Mathew's death was devastating, leaving her with the burden of running the farm while caring for her young children. No doubt it was a comfort to have her brother-in-law's family next door, but that proximity would lead to tragedy a year later when cholera struck the community.

Cholera was a scourge in America in the mid-nineteenth century. Though often associated with the cramped conditions of urban tenements, farming towns in the Midwest were not immune. Little was known at the time of the infectious nature of the disease, and the drinking water in Wilton would not have been particularly sanitary. "Water sources and sewage disposal were positioned for convenience, not safety—often so close together that the odor and taste of drinking water was a problem."[106] The disease was unmerciful, striking with speed, with symptoms frequently developing within hours of exposure, and often led to a painful death from severe diarrhea and dehydration. A person could seem fine in the morning and be dead the next day.

On August 31, 1869, Michael and Ann's son Felix (age nine) was the first Nugent child to die from cholera, followed a week later by Thomas (age four) and three weeks later by Mary Jane (age ten). On the farm next door, Catherine's oldest boy, John (age sixteen), fell ill and died on October 5, followed by his sister Lizzie (age eight) and their cousin Margaret (age one) on October 6. The disease continued to work its way through both households, and the next day, young Mathew (the newborn) died, followed by his brother Thomas (age fifteen) and sister Bridget (age nine) on October 10. Catherine's last surviving child, James (age three), perished on October 23, and his three-year old cousin Ann succumbed on November 19. They are all buried at Mt. Olivet Cemetery in Wallingford, Illinois, next to Mathew Nugent.

Twelve previously healthy children died within twelve weeks, completely wiping out one family (save the mother) and killing five of the seven children of another. With their farm on the eastern side of the township, John's family was spared.

It is inconceivable how Catherine held up during this overwhelming tragedy, but somehow, she endured. She inherited the farm after Mathew's death, and in 1872 she married Peter Brunner, a Swiss-born farmer eighteen years her junior, who farmed the land and added his own eighty-acre plot to the holdings.

Despite the hardships and tragedies, the extended Nugent family remained in Wilton, and there are still farms owned by Nugents today, especially in the northwest corner of the township, where Michael and Mathew first settled. The connection to the land, a passion inherited from Francis Nugent back in Ireland, buoyed by their faith, upheld them during these difficult times.

Back in Massachusetts, Felix Nugent, the only sibling who remained in New England, also took to farming, moving his family in 1853 from West Boylston to neighboring Clinton, another mill town that was fast becoming a hub for Irish immigrants.

Clinton, like Woods Hole, remained a small farming community for several centuries after its founding in 1654. Life centered on a small gristmill, which evolved into industrial mills. The Nashua River was an abundant source of water power, and by the 1850s, Clinton was home to a number of textile mills, most famously, the Bigelow Carpet Mill, owned by brothers Erastus and Horatio Bigelow. As a child, Erastus Bigelow left school for factory work at age ten when his father's fortunes soured. He maintained that education was critical for personal advancement and for successful commerce. "As a means of high production efficiency, it should be made possible for every individual to acquire a good general education, directed with a view to invigorate the body, elevate the moral faculties, and strengthen the intellectual powers, or, in other words, to fit the individual for the general duties of life."[107] He was one of the founders of the now world-renowned Massachusetts Institute of Technology, the same MIT that was instrumental in establishing the scientific community in Woods Hole.

The influx of so many newcomers created an opportunity for the Bigelow brothers to mold a community in their particular vision. Clinton, previously little more than a village, rapidly outpaced the growth of the surrounding region, and in 1850 it broke away from the mostly rural town of Lancaster. Town leadership had control over its civic amenities, but the Bigelow brothers were prepared to finance the critical services of the breakaway town of Clinton. The area was a blank slate, with rudimentary schools, no fire department and few shops. Erastus and Horatio Bigelow envisioned a community with good schools, a library, a fire department and wholesome entertainment. Like Joseph Story Fay in Woods Hole, the Bigelow brothers imagined how conditions could be improved and set about remaking the town.

By the time the Nugents arrived in Clinton in 1853, the town was already transforming. The same Nashua River that powered the mills also deposited on the surrounding land the rich loamy soil valued by farmers. Felix Nugent bought land on South Main Street, and there he had a small farm. He also opened a grocery, serving the burgeoning population of mill workers. He bought several commercial buildings in Clinton, built his family a house, served as an assessor of the town and was an overseer of the poor, an important civic position established in most New England towns to supervise

Felix Nugent's farm, photographed in 1897 by John L. Hildreth, to record existing buildings during the Wachusett Dam project. *Massachusetts Metropolitan Water Board.*

poor relief (money, food and clothing) for those in need. Having arrived with nothing, he became a pillar of Clinton society.[108]

Felix's Irish-born wife, Margaret, was kept busy raising the children. She gave birth to fifteen children, though only eight survived past the age of nine. The oldest son, William H. Nugent, was a grocer like his father and later served on the board of selectman. He is described as a "well known businessman" in the local historical documentation of the town, written in 1895. He never married and died only a few years after his father.

HELENA C. NUGENT, KNOWN to her family as Nellie, was born on January 24, 1875, in Clinton. The youngest of Felix and Margaret Nugent's many children, she was born twenty-five years after her oldest brother, so the age gap between the older children and the two youngest (Gertrude was two years her senior) was significant. No doubt this contributed to the close bond Helena and Gertrude shared throughout their lives.

Older brother James L. Nugent directly affected Helena's future, as his two oldest children became central characters in her life. James was a baker, and with his new bride, Margaret "Maggie" Murphy, he headed to Illinois to seek his fortune in 1887. James Edward Nugent was born in 1888, and eighteen months later, Grace Margaret Nugent was born. Then tragedy struck. In August 1890, Maggie died in Chicago, quite possibly in childbirth. Her body was transported to Massachusetts, where she was buried in Clinton.

James found himself alone, a widower with two young children, so he moved back to Clinton to live with his parents. In 1893, he married Celia Dorney of Springfield, twenty years his junior, and they had at least five children together. As James was rebuilding a family for himself, his older children from his first wife, James and Grace, were living next door with their paternal grandparents, Felix and Margaret. They were very young children and bonded with Gertrude and Helena, who was a schoolteacher and still living at home. For the next fifty years, in Woods Hole and Boston, James and Grace would weave in and out of the lives of Gertrude and Helena.

By 1895, the Nugents were well established in Clinton, and immigrants continued to stream into the big cities. Boston's population had been exploding for half a century, and the need for plentiful and clean water was a growing concern. That year, the Massachusetts state legislature established the Metropolitan Water Board, with the mission to "construct, maintain and operate a system of water works substantially in accordance with the plans and recommendations of the State Board of Health"[109] to supply water to the towns within ten miles of Boston.

The plan would combine water from the Nashua River in Clinton with the existing supply provided by the Sudbury and Cochituate systems closer to Boston. This required building a dam in Clinton to create a reservoir and then transporting water to the Boston area via aqueduct. The resulting Wachusetts Reservoir would cover two square miles, and effectively "drown out" parts of Clinton, Boylston and West Boylston with nearly eight billion gallons of water. The project was a massive undertaking, requiring the relocation of (and compensation for) farms, schools, factories and churches, with complex engineering challenges that come with building what was, at the time, the world's largest gravity dam.

One of the most difficult and delicate aspects of the project involved relocating the Roman Catholic cemetery. "By the 1890s St. John's Cemetery contained over three thousand bodies and was poised quite close to the margin of the new Reservoir. Preliminary engineering investigations indicated that the proposed flow line of the Wachusetts Reservoir would necessarily run through part of Clinton's Catholic cemetery. Ultimately it was decided to purchase the entire property from the archdiocese in Springfield. Extensive negotiations over price, replacement property and sensitivity to disturbing over three thousand graves were conducted between the Board and the Archbishop. Agreement was reached in 1898, the work completed by 1902, and final settlement made in 1910."[110]

The preparation that preceded relocation of the cemetery resembled nothing short of a military campaign. Harold Parker, chief engineer of the St. John's Catholic Cemetery Association, was tasked with the move. Detailed surveys were conducted, accounting for the location and orientation of each body and all markers, including headstones, footstones, cornerstones and memorials. The new St. John's Cemetery, located in neighboring Lancaster, was laid out in the same pattern as the old one, and the Consecration Monument originally erected in 1876 was set in the center of the new space. Minutely detailed daily records were kept in triplicate and stored in three secure locations at the end of each day to avoid any possible loss of information.

The Cemetery Association allowed "lot owners" or relatives of the deceased to attend the relocation of their loved ones, assuring families that everything was done correctly. At least five of Felix and Margaret's deceased children were part of this massive relocation, and the family plots are in

A Clinton family attending the exhumation and reinterring of loved ones during the cemetery relocation, while work continues in the foreground. *Massachusetts Metropolitan Water Board.*

Section E, at the heart of the cemetery. By 1902, 3,902 bodies had been exhumed and reinterred in the new cemetery. To Harold Parker's credit, not one body was misplaced.

However, the cemetery relocation project was not without challenges. Just as the planning and negotiations were underway, Reverend Patterson, pastor of St. John's Church, died suddenly. He was replaced in 1896 by Reverend John J. O'Keefe, and the ensuing proceedings were not as smooth as one might hope.

The Metropolitan Water Board entered into an agreement with the St. John's Catholic Cemetery Association, and Father O'Keefe was allowed to participate only as an ex officio member, with limited authority, for the church cemetery did not belong to the church itself. In an unusual arrangement, it was managed by a small group of parishioners who made up the Cemetery Association. For more than ten years, O'Keefe pushed back against what he considered an unorthodox situation, frequently addressing this issue in his sermons. And for more than ten years, the

Cemetery Association refused to turn over the cemetery, holding up the release of funds from the state and ultimately demanding that O'Keefe be transferred to another parish. As these disputes dragged on, it meant not only that final payment could not be made by the board but also that the cemetery remained unconsecrated. The bishop finally transferred O'Keefe to a parish in Dalton, Massachusetts, in 1910, at which point the cemetery was handed over to the new pastor, a native Clintonian, Father Michael Kittredge.

Father O'Keefe was well-meaning and positively influenced many aspects of Clinton life. Like the Bigelow brothers fifty years earlier, he believed that education and skills were vital components of a life well lived. During his fifteen years at St. John's, O'Keefe focused on improving the condition of the Irish mill workers, especially the women. He purchased property, using his own personal funds, to establish the "Guild House" on Union Street, in the center of town. "There he offered classes for women in sewing, cooking, home making, shorthand and typewriting. Unfortunately, much to the dismay of the pastor, women did not flock to take the classes or instruction of any kind. In O'Keefe's mind—and he wasn't shy about saying so from the altar—women would 'rather go to dances, hang around High Street, or sit in the Central Park.'"[111]

Father O'Keefe frequently used the pulpit to broadcast his disdain for the vices of Clinton's citizens. "He once went to the police station to announce that he had followed a beer wagon on Burditt Hill and had actually witnessed delivery of several cases of beer, noting the homes and demanding that the cops take action."[112] This stance was not universally popular. He purchased land to establish a boys' club, upgraded the facilities for the Catholic school and purchased the Bigelow home to serve as a convent for the sisters who taught there. On special feast days, he would lead the congregation of two thousand parishioners through the streets of Clinton, stopping to sing hymns and recite the rosary along the route as a public display of faith.

Father O'Keefe was also instrumental in helping the next wave of immigrants adapt to life in America. At the turn of the twentieth century, thousands of Polish families were fleeing imperial oppression on the Russian border and, like the Irish before them, looking for landownership and economic opportunity. Many were drawn to Clinton, attracted by the ample factory work. Few spoke English, which created hardships in daily life and also hampered their ability to participate fully in worship. The Catholic newcomers "were anxious to organize

The controversial pastor of St. John's Catholic Church in Clinton, Massachusetts, from 1898 to 1910, Father John J. O'Keefe. His portrait still hangs in the church office. *Sheehy Collection*.

a Polish parish as soon as possible, so that they could praise God and hear the word of God in their own native Polish tongue."[113] As members of St. John's Parish, they approached O'Keefe to request "a Polish priest to hear confessions and give sermons in their native tongues."[114] O'Keefe facilitated a meeting with the bishop, who agreed to assign Father Cyran as curate in St. John's Parish. The Polish congregation flourished, establishing a new church, the Parish of Our Lady of Jasna Gora, on Franklin Street in 1913. As the church population waned over the next century and parishioners assimilated to their new country, the parish merged back with St. John's in 2010 to form St. John the Guardian of Our Lady.

Father O'Keefe was a central figure in Clinton and also central in the life of the Nugents. Felix Nugent was a founder of the St. John's Temperance Society, organized by church members to oppose the consumption of alcoholic beverages, which no doubt strengthened the bond between the two teetotaling Irishmen. Helena's sister Gertrude lived in the rectory on Chestnut Street,[115] working as a servant for the priest's household before her promotion to housekeeper. She also found a position for her nephew James as a laborer at the rectory. So devoted was Gertrude to her employer that she left Clinton in 1910 and continued as O'Keefe's housekeeper when he was abruptly forced out and transferred to St. Agnes Church in Dalton, in western Massachusetts. Gertrude's mother had died the previous year, and she brought her niece Grace with her to live there as a servant.

During his time in Clinton, Father O'Keefe buried Felix (1904) and his wife, Margaret (1909), as well as their two oldest children, Mary (1901) and William (1906). He also performed the marriage of Helena Nugent to Walter Nickerson of Woods Hole at St. John's Catholic Church in 1903 and presumably oversaw Walter's conversion to the Catholic faith. At this point, the worlds of the Nugents, the Nickersons and the O'Keefes became inextricably entwined, and without these important relationships, the house on Millfield Street might not have been built.

# A House Is Built
## and Storms Are Brewing

Reverend John J. O'Keefe's early life was not dissimilar to Helena Nugent's. His parents, Thomas and Bridget O'Keefe, arrived in America in 1848 with very little, and yet the O'Keefe family touched the lives of thousands of people, as both the oldest and youngest sons became priests. Between them, John and Thomas O'Keefe were responsible for the souls of nearly five thousand Catholics in the Worcester area. Both brothers went beyond providing the guidance and rites necessary for a healthy spiritual life; they also strived to elevate the aesthetic within their respective communities. John focused on community buildings and activities that provided self-improvement opportunities and civic engagement. Thomas endeared himself to his congregants by focusing on beautification of his church and the cemetery adjacent. Far beyond the effect these two men had on Helena Nugent and Walter Nickerson, they left a legacy of inspired improvement.

The O'Keefes settled in Monson, a factory town near Worcester, and while raising nine children, Bridget O'Keefe involved herself in the religious development of the community. She helped establish worship space in a mill storeroom, offered up by the factory owners. "Catholic families were few in the area, but a large body of Catholic men were employed in building the New London and Northern Railroad. About sixty Catholics attended Mass. For some it was the first time they had seen a priest, or attended Mass, since they left their homes in Ireland."[116] Bridget O'Keefe was on hand to welcome the first priest to town.

After finishing school at age thirteen, John J. O'Keefe went to work in the woolen mills. His life was destined to change dramatically, however, when the church sent him to school in Nicolet, Canada, and then to St. Joseph's Seminary in Troy, New York. He was ordained a Catholic priest in 1875 at the robust age of thirty-three. For the next twenty years, Father O'Keefe served at various parishes around Springfield and Worcester before landing in Clinton in 1896. His sister Mary was his companion and housekeeper throughout this time until her death in 1908.

A few years after John's ordination, his youngest brother, Thomas, also escaped the mills and entered the College of the Holy Cross, graduating in 1886. Holy Cross was established in Worcester in 1843, even before the influx of Irish immigrants, as a training ground for Catholic priests, and the need for priests continued to rise throughout the nineteenth century. Just as his sister Mary had accompanied John to his various parishes, Thomas's sister Ellen became his companion. By 1894, Father Thomas O'Keefe had found his way back to Monson and was appointed pastor at St. Patrick's, the parish where he had grown up, serving there for the next fifty-three years.[117]

During his years in Clinton, Father John J. O'Keefe invested his personal funds in local real estate, creating civic programs to improve the lives of Clinton's women and youth. He understood the opportunities that real estate could provide, and a few years after he left Clinton, at the age of seventy-four, O'Keefe completed an unusual real estate transaction for Helena Nugent Nickerson, one that would change her life and fortunes, as well as those of her sister Gertrude. In October 1916, in Dalton, O'Keefe agreed to loan $10,000 to Helena, in a formal mortgage document witnessed by Gertrude. On the same day in Falmouth, Walter Nickerson added Helena to the Millfield house deed so that the loan agreement could be written between the priest and Helena, with Walter playing a secondary role in the financial transaction.

By 1922, just five years after the house was complete, Father O'Keefe's health had begun to decline, and in November of that year, exhibiting financial savvy (though tempting fate with his advanced age), he assigned the mortgage over to his brother Father Thomas O'Keefe in exchange for one dollar. Just four months later, Father John died at his brother's home in Monson, not far from where he had grown up. Father Thomas honored his brother by erecting a stone archway in Bethany Cemetery, where Father John is buried along with most of his family.

In May 1923, the final piece of the puzzle fell into place. Having lost her job and her home in one fell swoop with the death of her employer, Gertrude went to stay with her sister in Woods Hole. In May, Father Thomas O'Keefe assigned the mortgage for the house on Millfield over to Gertrude, again for one dollar.[118] This generous and carefully orchestrated act guaranteed the financial well-being of both Gertrude and Helena and cemented a sisterly bond that went well beyond their ownership of the house.

Walter and Helena Nickerson were active in Woods Hole life. A convert to Catholicism, Walter embraced his faith with deep devotion, and he joined the Knights of Columbus in Falmouth. St. Joseph's Catholic Church, located just across the street from the new house on Millfield Street, provided a social outlet with regular whist games (a precursor to bridge), especially welcome during the dreary winter months. Helena frequently earned the top score in whist, while Walter made the newspaper in 1920 for the ignominious distinction of having the lowest score of the evening.

Little Joseph Nickerson had a few moments of *Enterprise* fame of his own when the April 1, 1916 edition recapped his seventh birthday party. "Joseph N. Nickerson, son of Mr. & Mrs. Walter Nickerson, celebrated his seventh birthday last Saturday. Eleven of his little playmates were entertained at his home from 2:30 to 5:30 o'clock. The time was spent playing games and a collation was served."[119]

Three years later, Joseph was featured again after "a narrow escape from drowning last Monday evening, when he fell out of a boat into the Eel pond. He was rescued by Rev. Fr. T.F. Kennedy [of St. Joseph's] after he had gone down twice. He swallowed a considerable quantity of water, but now has recovered from the effects of the unfortunate experience."[120] It's odd that the son of a seaman like Walter wasn't an outstanding swimmer, but perhaps it was a rough day. This incident was republished multiple times over the years in the "Once Upon A Time" feature of the *Enterprise*, high drama on the pond. Perhaps it struck a chord with the locals, of whom "it was said, you had to fall in the pond to belong to Woods Hole."[121]

Woods Hole became the maypole around which the Nugents and Nickersons danced, weaving in and out of the village during summers and holidays, then taking off for varying points around New England, before returning again to reconnect. Following her parents' messy divorce, Gladys Bunker went to live with her aunt Clara, first in Keene, New Hampshire, where Ernest had taken a job, and then in Auburn, New York, home of the Dunn & McCarthy Shoe Company. Elizabeth Bunker remained in Woods Hole with Florence until they both moved back to Washington, D.C., near the end of World War I, securing one of the plentiful civil service jobs available in the city. Grace and James Nugent also circled around Woods Hole, frequently staying with Helena and Gertrude.

Ice skaters on Eel Pond in the 1940s. The Nickerson House is to the right of center. *WHHM.*

The year 1917 was momentous for Woods Hole and the world beyond. In April, the Unites States officially entered World War I. Evidence of the war effort abounded in Falmouth, considered a vulnerable spot as German U-boats trolled the seaboard. Indeed, there were several physical encounters between civilians and submarines off the coast. If Chief Brody struggled to get visitors into the water in Amity after the shark attacks in *Jaws*, imagine the efforts required to get people to go to the beach after tourists were attacked by a U-boat in Orleans in 1918.[122] Throughout the country, the government called for no-meat Mondays and wheatless Wednesdays as a means to support the war effort, and everyone was expected to do his or her part. In the midst of this chaos, the house on Millfield Street was completed.

Conflict of a different sort consumed the family that fall. Walter's sister Minnie, who never married and often traveled the Northeast visiting family, went to see Clara in Auburn, New York. She created quite a stir when she "surprised her family by returning to the [Woods Hole] home of her brother, Alfred"[123] unexpectedly. But why did she flee New York? From outward appearances, nothing seemed amiss with Clara and Ernest. They continued to maintain a residence in Cambridge, listed together in the city directory until his death there in 1931. But their lives were not as calm as they pretended.

In reality, Ernest was living a double life. He began an affair in Keene, New Hampshire, with Grace Loveland, a married mother of three, who divorced her husband just as Ernest was leaving his job there. It took some creative research to uncover that Ernest and Grace were living together in St. Louis in 1920 and 1930, Ernest still earning a living in the shoe business. All this was happening while Clara and Ernest were still married and, on paper at least, living together in Boston.

Research indicates that Grace Loveland moved to Auburn around the same time the Nutters moved there. She was living a short distance from Clara and Ernest, and the affair must have been intense. Although they did not formally divorce, Clara and Ernest went their separate ways, he to Missouri and she to Cambridge. When Grace died in 1947, her obituary in the *St. Louis Dispatch* referred to her as the "dear wife of the late Ernest Nutter,"[124] suggesting a long and traditional marriage. But her death certificate tells a different story, listing her spouse as Edward Loveland, the husband she divorced in 1913. That fact suggests that she was never legally married to Ernest, living as a common-law wife, while Clara chose to carry on as before, living independently in Boston and ignoring—publicly, at least—the betrayal.

Minnie had always been close to Clara, visiting her sister in Boston, Salem and Auburn. It is likely that Minnie's unexpected return to Woods Hole in 1917 was tied to the stressful circumstances of Clara's unraveling marriage in Auburn. When Clara relocated to Eliot Street in Cambridge, Minnie went to live with her and remained there until her death in 1926. She is buried in the family plot in Woods Hole.

Clara remained in Cambridge for a decade, moving back to the Cape in the 1930s. She lived in Sandwich as a housekeeper before moving to a nursing home in Bourne. She died in 1960 at age ninety, and the last surviving child of Oliver and Mary Nickerson is buried alongside her parents in Woods Hole.

Clara's niece Gladys (Nettie's adopted daughter) was living with her when the Nutter marriage blew apart. By the end of 1917, Gladys had married Aden J. King, a promising young chemist, moving with him to Syracuse, New York. Aden earned a doctorate, specializing in radiological research and producing several patents. Gladys and Aden had one daughter, Mary King, and the small family made frequent visits to Woods Hole over the years. They clearly were happy there, as one hundred years later, Gladys's grandchildren were still living in Woods Hole.

Another tragedy struck in December 1917, when Kathryn Gifford, the wife of Walter's nephew Waldo, died at Nettie's home in Washington, D.C. Waldo moved back to Boston and two years later married Emily Frances McClennan, who was also widowed in 1917, leaving her with two daughters.

Gladys Bunker King and her husband, Dr. Aden J. King, in Woods Hole. Date unknown. *WHHM.*

Waldo worked as an accountant at H.P. Hood & Sons, the New England dairy icon. After twelve years of marriage, at age thirty-nine, Emily gave birth to a son, Gerald Riley Gifford, one of only two known blood-related great-grandchildren of Oliver and Mary Nickerson.

DESPITE THE WAR, DEATH, and discord, Walter and Helena must have been thrilled to finally move into their big house on Eel Pond in 1917. Though chilly in the winter, theirs was an elegant house, even if Walter chose to keep his lobster traps stacked up along the seawall. By 1919, the naval presence had waned in Woods Hole, and life returned to its prewar calm, with whist games and concerts punctuating the Nickersons' routine. A few years passed before Helena's sister Gertrude moved in, just as fourteen-year-old Joseph Nickerson was leaving home to enter St. Anselm's School in Manchester, New Hampshire. St. Anselm's, a Benedictine college and preparatory school, was established in 1889 as a liberal arts college and training ground for priests. The prestigious boarding school was attended by elite New England men, such as Joseph's classmate and future U.S.

senator Thomas J. Dodd. Joseph returned to Woods Hole during holidays, but his time at home was limited.

In the early 1920s, as Gertrude settled into the house on Eel Pond and Joseph settled into school, Walter's health declined. Several times, his appearance "on the sick list" was mentioned in the *Enterprise*, along with news of who was renting his Crow Hill house and the results of various card games.

# 1925–1945

In 1925, life changed forever for Helena, Joseph and Gertrude. On February 12, at the age of fifty-seven, Walter E. Nickerson died at New England Deaconess Hospital in Boston of complications from surgery for pancreatic cancer. The newspaper announced, "The town has again lost another of its good citizens, Mr. Walter Nickerson. Services were held in the Catholic church here, interment being in Clifton [*sic*], Mass. Mr. Nickerson is survived by a widow, one son, two brothers and five sisters."[125] Unfortunately, there was no formal obituary for Walter to shed light on his life and interests. The Knights of Columbus approved a Resolution of Condolences, "praying for the repose of his soul, that he may enjoy that infinite happiness to which we firmly believe his honesty, charity and devotion to our Holy religion, and his consistent discharge of his whole duty in all the relations of his life entitle him."[126]

Joseph was at school at the time, and according to his niece Mary Byrne Ramsbottom, his mother would not allow Joseph to interrupt his studies to come home for the funeral. He was just shy of sixteen at the time and had been extremely close with his father. Prior to his father's death, to show his admiration for the man, Joseph changed his middle name from Nugent to Walter, so the death of his father must have been difficult, especially at such a distance. His mother placed a letter in the newspaper from the two of them, extending their "heartfelt appreciation and thanks for the sympathy extended by the Knights of Columbus and our many friends, and for the flowers which were sent during our great sorrow."[127] But Joseph was left to mourn from afar.

Because Joseph was a minor, Helena's nephew James Nugent became his official guardian, and they remained close throughout their lives. Walter died without leaving a will, so Helena became the executor of his estate. In addition to the house on Millfield, which Walter and his wife owned jointly, Walter left one "26 ft. lobster boat—1 old dory—80 lobster pots and 1 dwelling house," the house on Middle Street. Following his father's death,

Joseph remained at school, earning his academic diploma from the prep school in 1926 and going on to get his bachelor's in 1930.

His guardian, James, moved to Boston, securing a position at the Loose-Wiles Biscuit Company. His father was a baker, so perhaps this inspired him, though young James entered the baking business from the financial end, rising to bookkeeper within a few years. The Loose-Wiles Biscuit Company was the world's largest baker at the time, and James remained with the company for decades, becoming a cost accountant in the sales office by the time it changed its name to Sunshine Biscuits in 1946. In 1925, he married Blanche Ferguson, a dressmaker and fellow Catholic six years his senior, and for a short time, Grace, working as a secretary, lived with them before they moved to an apartment at 72 Westland Avenue in the 1930s.

Following Walter's death in 1925, things changed significantly for Helena. For a few years, she remained in Woods Hole and immersed herself in church activities. She and Gertrude were charter members of the local chapter of the Daughters of Isabella, the female auxiliary of the Knights of Columbus, started in Falmouth in 1925, with Helena serving as financial secretary that first year.[128] In 1927, she retreated to Clinton, where several family members still lived, and accepted a position teaching at the Lancaster Industrial School for Girls, just a few miles from where she had grown up.

She continued to spend her summers in Woods Hole with Gertrude, teaching in Lancaster and renting her Woods Hole properties during the off-season. In 1931, Gertrude came to the Lancaster Industrial School for Girls as an assistant matron, a position she would hold for the next fifteen years. She arrived at the school just as Helena was leaving, headed to Boston to live with Grace.

During the winter months of the 1930s, Helena shared a flat with her niece on Haviland Street in Boston. Grace suffered from ill health, and eventually had to give up her employment position. In the summer of 1937, Grace came to Woods Hole for a visit, and on July 11, she died at Cape Cod Hospital following a heart attack. She is buried alongside her Nugent family and her uncle Walter at St. John's Cemetery in Lancaster.

The years following Grace's death were as tumultuous as any Woods Hole had experienced to date. Major events were affecting Cape Cod and people around the world, including weather, the changing economy and a looming war.

The first momentous event took place September 21, 1938, when a Category 3 hurricane was mis-forecast by the Washington, D.C. weather bureau and slammed into New England unannounced. The storm was one of the most destructive ever to hit New England, and the damage in Falmouth was significant. The hurricane arrived on a Wednesday, and despite the chaos, the *Falmouth Enterprise* put out an issue of the newspaper on Friday the twenty-third, relaying in excruciating detail the personal stories of danger and loss affecting the region.

The storm blew in at 4:00 p.m., and "by 5:45 the entire main street of Woods Hole, School street, Millfield street, Spencer Baird road, and Penzance road were flooded."[129] As the water continued to rise, the force of the storm washed away the drawbridge as the water from Woods Hole Harbor poured into Eel Pond. "Men rowed across Main street and Eel pond to Millfield street where the surging tide was lapping at the front of St. Joseph's church and rectory."[130] Millfield Street was especially hard-hit, as it bore the brunt of water pushed into the harbor by the rising current.

In Dr. Oliver Strong's firsthand recollection, written immediately following the storm, he referenced the damage to Millfield several times: "All the low land of Woods Hole was overflowed…[the] baseball field, Gardiner Road, Millfield Street…eight feet of water on it.…A young man swimming (or rowing) in a yard on Millfield Street struck something submerged and found it was the top of an automobile.…Practically all houses more or less filled with water, even though intact and not moved."[131]

The hurricane produced storm tides of fourteen to twenty-five feet in various spots across New England, hitting the Rhode Island coast especially hard. In just a few hours, every cottage that sat on Napatree Point, near Watch Hill, Rhode Island, was washed out to sea.[132] In Woods Hole, the wind meter at Nobska Point broke at 127 knots. The winds pushed the water from Great Harbor into Buzzards Bay with tremendous force, and it had nowhere to go, circling back and over the low point of land at the causeway separating Penzance Point from the rest of Woods Hole. The surge reversal cut off the peninsula from the village and swept several local men to their deaths. One of them was William Briggs, caretaker of one of the large estates on Penzance Point, and the grandfather of Rob Blomberg, the Woods Hole tour guide. Briggs had been moving oriental carpets to the second floor of one of the large homes and was not expecting water to come from the north. His body was found by Prosser Gifford the next day amid the storm detritus.

By the time the hurricane moved into Canada several hours later, five people in Woods Hole had died, including three Coast Guard members who had been assisting with the rescue efforts. Most of the homes along the water were badly damaged, if not destroyed. The basement of the Nickerson House was completely flooded, but the house survived. When the hurricane hit Woods Hole, most of the summer residents had departed, and while Helena had spent the summer on the Cape, she was not there during the storm itself. The family, including her son Joseph and his fiancée, Frances, along with her nieces, arrived to assess the damage (including young Mary, my mother-in-law's friend).[133]

The portrayal in the news of widespread destruction from the storm greatly concerned summer residents. Over the next few weeks, a number of them returned to Woods Hole to assess the damage to their properties and commiserate with the year-round residents. For the most part, the grand houses, situated on higher ground, were fine, though many boathouses and yachts set along the shore were flooded, damaged or washed away. By contrast, most of the year-round residents saw their homes and businesses devastated.

Theodore H. Brown, summer resident and Boston insurance executive, recognized the plight of the year-round residents and organized an effort to solicit contributions in support of those who lost property or were financially devastated by the storm. "He sent letters to those who spend their summers on Penzance Point, at Nobska, Gansett, Buzzards Bay shore, Crow Hill, and the village. The replies and contributions must have been gratifying, for

Joseph and Frances Nickerson, taken around the time of their wedding (and shortly after the 1938 hurricane). Behind them is the Angelus Bell Tower in the Mary Garden, across from St. Joseph's Church. *Ramsbottom Collection.*

Mr. Brown soon called upon a few prominent Woods Hole businessmen to assist him in preparing a list of those persons who lost property or who were materially and financially damaged by the storm."[134]

A few days before Christmas, Brown, accompanied by Sergeant Arthur F. Hamilton and Patrolman Wright, visited the homes of nearly fifty year-round residents, presenting them with a "Christmas card containing several crisp bank notes [and] conveyed the sympathetic understanding and cheering best wishes of Woods Hole summer residents for those whose homes were damaged by the storm and flood during the September 21 hurricane."[135] Brown made it clear that this was not charity but that "he simply wanted the people of Woods Hole to realize that the summer residents with whom they have been so friendly thought of them in their distress and wished to assist those who had suffered most by brightening Christmas."[136]

The aftermath of the Hurricane of 1938 was almost as trying to the people of Woods Hole as the storm itself. With the drawbridge washed out, the only way to get to the lower end of Main Street (now Water Street) was to go around Eel Pond. Samuel T. Cahoon complained that "the most dangerous corners in Woods Hole are Main and School street, School street and Millfield street, Millfield street and West street—the route people must follow to reach the other side of the bridge by automobile. It is bad enough now and will be worse when summer comes."[137] Millfield was seven feet narrower than standard roads in the area, and there was a great deal of concern over the safety of extra traffic. Villagers were also concerned about the loss of business, the need for extra police protection around the temporary footbridge and even danger from fires if the fire trucks could not get through.

Somehow, Woods Hole made it through that first summer, and by December 1939, construction for a new drawbridge was underway. It cost $68,688, of which the Town of Falmouth paid half—the state picked up the other half—and once the funding was approved, the process to rebuild moved quickly. The first car drove over the new drawbridge on June 4, 1940, just hours after the painters were "applying final touches to the heavy red lead-based paint."[138]

It had been suggested that the massive storm that hit in 1938 was the cause for the significant "drooping" of the northeast corner of the Millfield house. However, there are reasons to believe the damage occurred sixteen years later when Cape Cod was clobbered with a one-two punch from Hurricanes Carol and Edna in 1954.

Hurricane Carol was a Category 3 storm that made landfall on August 31 in Old Saybrook, Connecticut, about eighty miles to the west of Woods Hole, bringing with it one-hundred-mile-per-hour wind gusts and a ten-foot storm surge. Like the Hurricane of 1938, its arrival was unexpected—or at least, it hit earlier than expected—catching residents off-guard. And as happened in 1938, Millfield Street was completely underwater.

In true Yankee form, "most residents stuck to their guns and refused to leave their homes."[139] The resilience of the community was highlighted when the Landfall Restaurant, under four feet of water on Tuesday morning, managed to open its doors for business the following evening. "The sea swept through, taking most of the windows and buckling the floor. Personnel worked all day washing down the restaurant, kitchen, furniture and glasses, and Wednesday evening they served liquor but no food. This weekend, food will be served,"[140] declared David Estes, the owner. A portable piano was borrowed from a yacht that had been rescued the day before by the Coast Guard, and business was conducted by candlelight. "Mr. Estes said he was happy to have made a small demonstration that Falmouth doesn't call it quits in face of difficulties."[141]

Less than two weeks later, Hurricane Edna struck New England, and while it was only a Category 2 storm, it hit Woods Hole during high tide,

The Nickerson House on the right, with the Angelus Bell Tower peeking out, 1954. Note the large boat that came ashore during Hurricane Carol. *WHHM.*

adding six feet on top of the storm surge. Once again, Millfield Street was overwhelmed by the water. In December, Sidney and Josephine Lawrence, who owned the house at the time, filed for a tax abatement valued at $9,300, due to the excessive hurricane damage, which affected part of the first floor, the cellar and the roof.[142] More than likely, that storm damage contributed to the "droop" that affects the house to this day.

In October 1938, a month after the hurricane, Helena and Joseph added Gertrude to the deed of the Middle Street house. The following year, Gertrude discharged the mortgage the O'Keefes had assigned to her, and she was subsequently added to the Millfield Street deed, putting both houses in joint tenancy with her sister and nephew. The house was now mortgage free, but there was another issue looming: rising taxes.

In 1933, the house on Middle Street had a tax bill of $126, while the house on Millfield was taxed at $159, for a total annual tax of about $285. The tax figures, posted in the newspaper, put them in the top tier of Falmouth real estate taxpayers, alongside the owners of the grand "cottages" of summer residents. Two years later, the tax rose to around $337, and by the end of the decade it was $420.[143] The Nickersons were not wealthy people, and these costs must have caused anxiety each year when the tax bill came due. Helena's only source of income by then was renting the cottage on Middle Street and rooms in the house on Eel Pond.

Following the Great Hurricane of 1938, things were no calmer for the people of Woods Hole or the Nickersons. A few months after the storm blew through, Nettie Nickerson Bunker, Walter's independent sister, traveled from Woods Hole to Syracuse to be with her critically ill daughter, Elizabeth. She arrived just in time, as Elizabeth died on December 1 from chronic heart issues, leaving behind a husband and young daughter, Bruce and Rita Jetty. Just twenty-four hours later, Nettie died of a heart attack at her daughter's home. A double funeral was held at Church of the Messiah, and mother and daughter, separated from each other during much of Elizabeth's childhood, are buried side by side in Woods Hole Cemetery.

Nine months later, in September 1939, war broke out in Europe, and by the time the United States officially entered the conflict in December 1941, the U.S. Navy dominated Woods Hole. The navy presence in the village had been significant for decades, dating back to the establishment of U.S. Fisheries with support from the secretary of the navy. Woods Hole had much to offer the navy, including research and development, and Cape Cod required defensive capabilities, as it was a target of enemy forces dating back to the Revolutionary War. The German U-boat attack in 1918 marked the

*Above*: Twenty-four hours after Hurricane Carol blew through Woods Hole, the Landfall Restaurant (in background) reopened its doors to customers. *WHHM.*

*Opposite:* World War II draft registration card for Joseph Nickerson. *National Archives.*

SERIAL NUMBER **1054**

1. NAME (Print) JOSEPH WALTER NICKERSON
(First) (Middle) (Last)

ORDER NUMBER **787**

2. ADDRESS (Print) 4/25/42 : 72 Bayley street, Westwood, Mass.
12 NORMAN St CAMBRIDGE
(Number and street or R. F. D. number) (Town) Norfolk (County) MASS (State)
Middlesex

3. TELEPHONE Eli 0925
(Exchange) (Number)

4. AGE IN YEARS 31 yrs
DATE OF BIRTH March 24 1909
(Mo.) (Day) (Yr.)

5. PLACE OF BIRTH Clinton
(Town or county)
MASS
(State or country)

6. COUNTRY OF CITIZENSHIP
U.S.A.

7. NAME OF PERSON WHO WILL ALWAYS KNOW YOUR ADDRESS
MRS FRANCES BYRNE NICKERSON
(Mr., Mrs., Miss) (First) (Middle) (Last)

8. RELATIONSHIP OF THAT PERSON
WIFE

9. ADDRESS OF THAT PERSON
12 NORMAN St CAMBRIDGE MIDDLESEX MASS
(Number and street or R. F. D. number) (Town) (County) (State)

10. EMPLOYER'S NAME
DONNELLY NEON and ELECTRIC Co.

11. PLACE OF EMPLOYMENT OR BUSINESS
3190 Washington St JAMAICA Plain MIDDLESEX MASS
(Number and street or R. F. D. number) (Town) (County) (State)

I AFFIRM THAT I HAVE VERIFIED ABOVE ANSWERS AND THAT THEY ARE TRUE.

REGISTRATION CARD
D. S. S. Form 1 (over)

Joseph W Nickerson
(Registrant's signature)

first attack on the U.S. mainland since the War of 1812, and fear of a repeat attack was understandable for Cape Cod residents. Active shipping lanes running between Boston and New York required protection, and there was even a busy POW camp established at Camp Edwards (now Joint Base Cape Cod). Throughout World War II, U-boat attacks were of concern to the military and civilians alike, and the focus of military readiness was centered on Woods Hole.

"Woods Hole presented an unfamiliar picture," according to Paul Galtsoff in his 1962 lab history. "The Fisheries grounds and the adjacent buildings of the MBL were surrounded by high fence, and become inaccessible to civilians. The gay crowd that used to assemble near the aquarium and around the seal pool was no longer there. Less than half of the MBL laboratory rooms were occupied. Bright-looking pleasure boats were gone, and very few fishing vessels were seen in the harbor. Even the New Bedford-Nantucket steamer lost its smart appearance under a coat of gray paint. At night everything was pitch dark and the streets were deserted."[144]

In 1941, as Woods Hole transformed into a military outpost, Helena returned to the Lancaster Industrial School for Girls, accepting a position as a house matron. Gertrude, who had worked there for the past ten years, continued in her role of assistant matron until 1947. The sisters spent their summers in Woods Hole throughout the war, living in the house on Millfield and soaking in the sea air. Joseph Nickerson, by now an electrician with Donnelly Neon and Electric Company in Jamaica Plain, was living in Cambridge with his bride, Frances Byrne. Joseph registered for the draft, but he suffered from a variety of health issues and was never called to serve.

This is the point at which the most unsettling mystery to date emerged, one that has proven extremely challenging to resolve and was equally difficult to uncover. On the bottom of page 6A, the 1940 U.S. Census shows Joseph and Frances, both thirty-one years old, living at 12 Norman Street in Cambridge, matching the information on his draft card. But flipping to page 6B—done completely by chance—revealed another family member: Dorothy Nickerson, daughter, age fourteen.

Where on earth had Dorothy come from? Mary Ramsbottom confirmed that Joseph and Frances had no children, yet here was a fourteen-year-old daughter, Dorothy Nickerson, appearing out of nowhere. Who is Dorothy, and why are there no other references to her? The question had no easy answer, and the hunt for Dorothy continues.

In June 1945, Helena Nickerson opened her house on Millfield Street for one final summer. Though the war would not officially end until September 2, people were ready to return to normal, filling beach towns to capacity. The newspaper reported that "the 'season' started off last weekend with an ominous rush. There was foretaste of many crowded weekends, many stresses and strains. Stores were pressed to serve the stream of shoppers. Eating places were jammed early and late on Saturday and Sunday. Sunday morning the first breakfast-seeking throng of vacationists wandered fruitlessly up and down Main street. The weekend's heavy motor traffic continued into the week."[145] Beachgoers battled the "resident army and navy colony" for room on the sidewalks, locals complained about the influx of traffic, summer people complained about the shortage of city newspapers and vacationing Bostonians relished the cool air after a recent heat wave in the city.

So many people were flocking to Cape Cod that housing was difficult to find. The military was occupying hotels across the area, and the dearth of available rooms led some to advertise for help finding a place to live. "$50.00 Reward, For person who is able to obtain an unfurnished home for a family of six. Write Enterprise, Box C."[146] For those living in Falmouth today, this sounds all too familiar.

At the end of the summer, Helena, Joseph and Gertrude sold the house on Eel Pond to a wealthy New York financier, Edward A. Norman. A few days later, they sold the house on Middle Street to Charles Ofstrock, an agent at the Woods Hole Steamship Wharf, and his wife, Jean.

The era of the Nickersons of Millfield Street had come to an end.

## 13

# BOHEMIANS AT THE GATE

I n 1945, the world was in transition. The country was in transition. And the Nickerson House was in transition.

In September 1945, the house on Millfield Street was sold to Edward Albert Norman, a securities trader from New York City. Edward first came to Woods Hole in the 1920s, purchasing a cottage on Cross Street (now Bigelow Street) a week before the stock market crash of 1929. His wife, Dorothy, and their children, Andrew and Nancy, spent entire summers in Woods Hole, with Edward joining them for long weekends.

Society in towns like Falmouth took on a familiar rhythm in the summer. Children of the wealthy families spent the week enjoying freedom and adventure unavailable to them back home, roaming the beaches, learning to sail and mingling with the offspring of entrepreneurs and lobstermen alike. The wives took up gardening (with strong local men hired to help with the heavy chores), hosted teas and basked in the slower pace of life.

On the weekend, the village filled up with the husbands, who took the train from Boston or New York, arriving at the rail depot where today the ferries depart for the islands. Beginning in 1884, there was a subscription train that ran between Boston and Woods Hole from June through early October, bringing elite families (Forbes, Fays, even President Grover Cleveland) to their summer homes. Known as *The Flying Dude*, or Dude Train, this service ended in 1916, but the arrival of trains full of weekend husbands continued until train service to the area was discontinued in 1965.[147]

If the children set the pace for weekday life, the arrival of the men at the weekend shifted the focus to sailing, tennis and adult festivities. Dinner parties with the "right" people were a less formal extension of the high-society gatherings in the city—less stuffy, perhaps, but no less elite.

This was the world of Edward and Dorothy Norman. The family outgrew the small house purchased in 1929, and in 1935 Norman purchased the George B. Wilber estate on Penzance Point. Built before 1890, the "Wilbur house stands between the Jewett and Barlow estates. It has frontage both on Buzzards Bay and on Great Harbor where it has a boat house. There is also a chauffeur's cottage and a garage with quarters for a caretaker."[148] Norman quickly set about "reconditioning" the house at the grand cost of $16,000.[149] In 1936, the *Falmouth Enterprise* published an article about three large estates in Woods Hole undergoing renovations that year. With each project, no expense was spared, though varied efforts to maintain the original look were employed. With what could be interpreted as derision, the article suggests that the "Norman house presents an entirely new appearance. In its new form it is strictly a New England house, made somewhat unconventional by two porches at each side, and by the grouping of first floor front windows in two panels of three."[150]

The original house was "stripped of its dormers and porches—stripped indeed of everything except the very skeleton—before remodeling began." A tennis court was built behind a high fence, and "on rainy days the Normans and their friends will not have to bemoan the weather. One of the two boat-houses on the Buzzards Bay shore, which now juts out over the water, will be moved inland and converted into a playhouse with badminton facilities. The other boat-house, which contains a [marine] railway, will be sufficient for Mr. Norman's requirements. Incidentally, Mr. Norman is not planning to buy a large yacht. He swears by his faithful Herreshoff 'S' boat, the Gull."[151]

The irony, of course, is that these luxurious homes were sitting on a former guano "farm" where bird poop and fish guts were combined to create high-grade fertilizer. Just as the industrial hazard site was remade into an exclusive enclave for the well-bred and wealthy, Edward Norman himself was remade as an establishment scion. No doubt he benefited from his family's vast wealth, but his was new money and even a new name.

Aaron Nusbaum, Edward's father, epitomized the American entrepreneur success story. The Jewish son of German immigrants, Aaron was determined

The Dude Train making its way to the Woods Hole railroad depot. *Digital Commonwealth.*

to succeed in the business world. In 1893, he leveraged a relationship with Marshall Field, a member of the World's Fair planning commission, to secure the contract for soft drinks at the World's Columbian Exposition in Chicago. His profit for the summer was $150,000 (about $3.5 million today), and he invested that money in a pneumatic tube manufacturer, whose product was used to communicate between floors in department stores before telephones. During an 1895 sales meeting with Richard Sears, the cash-strapped department store co-founder offered to sell Nusbaum 50 percent of the company for $75,000. Nusbaum convinced his brother-in-law, Julius Rosenwald, to buy one-quarter of the company, and he purchased the other 25 percent. Nusbaum and Rosenwald were instrumental in implementing changes that led sales at Sears, Roebuck and Company to skyrocket from $800,000 in 1895 to $11 million in 1900.[152]

Nusbaum had a falling out with Sears and Rosenwald in 1901, and they bought him out for $1.25 million, creating a lifelong feud between Nusbaum and his sister's family but leaving him extremely wealthy. Nusbaum took his family on an extended trip to Europe, and on his return to the States, he changed his name to Aaron Norman. He founded a wealth investment firm, and his fortune continued to grow.

Young Edward grew up in this privileged world, born in Chicago and raised in New York City. He attended the New York Military Academy and then transferred and received his bachelor's degree in economics and sociology in 1923 from Harvard, where he was on the polo team, and enjoyed skiing and hunting. Though he maintained a strong interest in the Jewish settlements in Palestine in the 1920s, and many of his business interests supported Israel, he adapted well to the privileged life dominated by establishment WASPs.

In 1925, Edward married Dorothy Stecker, a Philadelphia socialite from a prominent Jewish family. Only twenty at the time of her marriage, Dorothy grew up in a world of extreme affluence and social connections. She spoke French and German and possessed the sophistication that comes from attending the best private schools, followed by a year at Smith College and another at the University of Pennsylvania. She honed her artistic tastes at the Barnes Collection in Philadelphia. She also developed a progressive mindset, immersing herself in liberal causes, she would later write, as a guilty reaction to her upbringing of wealth and privilege.

In addition to his financial activities, Edward served without pay as a research secretary for the Cooperative League, an organization that advanced the concept of enterprises that are jointly owned and democratically controlled. He was passionate about this cause, representing the Woods Hole Consumer Cooperative at national meetings. Dorothy focused on the American Civil Liberties Union (ACLU) and participated in Margaret Sanger's birth control crusade. She had a gift for connecting with people and causes, and much of her life was devoted to creating communities that rallied behind progressive efforts.

During her summers in Woods Hole, Dorothy indulged in the activities of the urban elite. She was a keen tennis player, winning the local championship in 1937; served as president of the Children's School of Science in 1939; and was a member of the Garden Club. She hosted and attended teas and parties with the other wealthy wives.

Edward Norman was an enthusiastic supporter of the Woods Hole Yacht Club and was elected its secretary/treasurer in 1930, recounted as "one of the most fortunate events for the yacht club's future development.... The Woods Hole Yacht Club had no official clubhouse for the first few years of operation. Mr. Frost and Mrs. Crane generously gave the club the use of their boats and docks. However, treasurer Norman recognized that the imposition to the families was a potentially serious problem and also that the growth of the yacht club could be hindered. At the annual meeting in 1932, he proposed the need for a yacht club independent of its neighbors' good will. He had searched for possible sites and found that property owned by the U.S. Government was not being used and possibly could be purchased."[153]

The bill of transfer was signed by President Roosevelt himself on June 25, 1935, as Norman headed to Europe on business. A local builder, H.V. Lawrence, was the principal contractor for the project, while Sidney Lawrence (to whom Norman would sell the house on Millfield Street in 1951) was tapped to construct the stone pier. Norman expected the project to be completed upon his return, but it was not. Apparently, there was confusion about funding and permits, which Edward methodically remedied in a matter of weeks. The new yacht club opened on August 27, 1935, to great fanfare. The entire history of the WHYC can be found in an article written by Edward Norman and published in the *Falmouth Enterprise* on May 13, 1938.[154] In wonderful detail, he addresses the perennial battle between the older and younger generations and the need to adapt to changing times, which reminds us that the times never do change that much.

Though Edward Norman was well-regarded by the community for his stewardship of the WHYC, that did not give him a free hand with the locals. In 1937, the Falmouth selectmen refused his request for a shellfish grant for the waters off his Penzance Point house. The rejection was front-page news:

> *So large was the attendance of objections that the hearing was transferred from the selectmen's office to the police station meeting room.*
>
> *"Every year someone on Penzance Point wants to do something to take away the rights of the people of Woods Hole," said Mr. Larkin. "It's a wonder to me that they haven't put up a stone wall across the road and harbor to keep us out of the district altogether. Roads, beaches, grants—they want everything."*[155]

In 1940, Edward Norman was elected commodore of the yacht club, but his seven-year term was interrupted by World War II. Though he had attended West Point before transferring to Harvard, in 1942 Edward decided to enter the navy, not the army. He "graduated as a lieutenant from the Navy's school of government at Columbia University and then served at sea for three years, most of the time on destroyer escorts in the Atlantic. He was attached to the staff of Admiral Stark, who commanded all Naval forces in the European theatre. Headquarters loaned him in 1945 to the Third Army of Gen. George Patton, where his knowledge of France and the language made him useful. He was with Patton's army when it invaded Germany. He became a lieutenant commander."[156] A month after the invasion, he was back in Woods Hole with his family.

Five months later, Norman purchased the Nickerson House on Millfield Street. It is unclear why he bought this property, though the protected

Lieutenant Commander Edward Norman in his navy uniform in New York City, 1942. *WHHM.*

harbor frontage must have appealed to him. He was a visionary, and perhaps he had a philanthropic purpose in mind for the house. It served mostly as a boardinghouse for the throngs of people occupying Woods Hole after the war. Whatever his long-term plans might have been, he did not see them through. In 1950, he leased the property to the Woods Hole Oceanographic Institution for summer housing. Under the auspices of Mrs. Wiley Sparks, who was in charge of all WHOI property, the house was transformed from a single-family home to a collection of boarding rooms. Nothing was substantially changed in the layout of the building, but a series of "improvements" were made to provide kitchen and living space to each of the newly arranged apartments on the first floor. The second and third levels were divided into ten separate bedrooms.[157] It was a new era for the house on Eel Pond.

The Normans held complex opinions on the merits of traditional versus modern architecture. In comparison to his home on Penzance Point, the house on Eel Pond was downright dowdy, but it had an authentic Cape Cod aesthetic that Norman appreciated. He took a stand against modern architecture in Woods Hole, vehemently opposing, for example, the new navy-funded building designed by E. Gunnar Peterson that was built at the end of Water Street. "It seems deplorable that Woods Hole should be further disfigured by the erection of the intended industrial structure."[158] Meanwhile, the general populace of Falmouth, in an unusual display of solidarity, embraced the construction of the practical building that would house WHOI's Laboratory for Oceanography. No doubt they appreciated the economic benefits it would bring to the town, and most of them did not look out their windows at it, unlike the elite residents on Penzance Point.

Yet back in New York City, Edward and Dorothy Norman embraced modern thinking and modern design. Their home at 124 East Seventieth Street, purchased in 1940, was completely gutted and redesigned by William Lescaze, a Swiss-born American architect and industrial designer, best known for pioneering modernism in American architecture. The four-story townhouse features a sleek façade, floor-to-ceiling windows facing the street and specially designed built-ins reflecting contemporary style. To this day, it is considered one of the best examples of modernist American residential design.

By 1951, the Norman marriage had fallen apart, and Edward Norman sold the house on Eel Pond to Sidney Lawrence, a Woods Hole stalwart. Though he kept his home on Penzance Point, Norman's final years were not happy. He entered into an unstable marriage in 1953 with Elizabeth

Cornell Blair, the fourth of her five husbands. Blair's daughter Hayden Herrera recounted a chaotic childhood in her memoir *Upper Bohemia* (2021), recalling the narcissistic yet art-filled pursuits of her parents, and her mother did not seem to mature during her brief marriage to Edward.

In October 1954, Edward Norman took a serious fall from a horse, fracturing his skull and requiring two brain surgeries. The following spring, he sold the Penzance Point house. The house was sold to Solene "Lucy" B. Lemann of New Orleans, whose family fortune came from selling their Louisiana salt farm to Morton Salt. Two months later, on June 20, Edward Albert Norman died at the home of a friend in New Canaan, Connecticut, and is buried in the Norman-Weill Cemetery in Katonah, New York.

Dorothy Norman transferred her affection for the sea to Long Island, spending summers there until her death in East Hampton in 1997 at age ninety-two. Her children, however, had established deep roots in Woods Hole, and a few years after their father's death, Nancy Norman Lassalle bought a house on Oyster Pond, while her brother Andrew Edward Norman purchased a studio barn nearby. Andrew and Nancy both continued to spend summers in Woods Hole until their deaths in 2004 and 2021, respectively.

# 14

# MODERN HISTORY

## *The Lawrences and Roslanskys*

Like Walter Nickerson, Sidney Lawrence was from an old Cape Cod family but a relative newcomer to Woods Hole. Lawrence bought dozens of properties around Falmouth, not all of them profitable transactions. Sidney and Josephine's primary residence was on Woods Hole Road, and the Millfield house was purchased as an investment. But real estate was only one of many ventures Sidney Lawrence embarked on in Woods Hole. His determination in the face of failure, his resilience and willingness to try everything to make a living mirror the economic grit of Woods Hole itself.

The Lawrence family had deep roots in the Upper Cape, dating back to the early eighteenth century. A distant Lawrence cousin who had accumulated massive wealth in the textile industry endowed the Lawrence Academy (1834) in Falmouth and the East End Meeting House (1797) in Hatchville. Solomon Lawrence, Sidney's father, owned a large farm in Teaticket, at the eastern end of Falmouth, raising dairy cows and selling the milk locally, in addition to growing crops. Solomon Lawrence died when Sidney was quite young, and as the oldest of six children, he was forced to leave school in the seventh grade to work the farm.[159]

Sidney continued to run the farm for many years and succeeded in putting all of his siblings through college in the process, quite an accomplishment in any era. After he married Josephine in 1904, Sidney sold the Teaticket farm and bought a house in Woods Hole. He purchased a fruit and vegetable shop on Eel Pond near the Candle House, and he used horse-drawn wagons, and then trucks, to deliver produce as far as North Falmouth. His next business involved buying a tract of land adjacent to his house on which he grew produce and built a pigsty, using garbage from the MBL mess hall to feed his pigs. Josephine was not a fan of the pigsty, and the porcine experiment ended when the smells from the pigsty became too much for her to bear.

Other business ventures included firewood delivery and running the Woods Hole Ice Co., with three large icehouses in Falmouth near Lakeview Avenue. He was described as "one of those know-how-to-make-do-with-almost-anything Cape Codders, and most of [his equipment] was homemade."[160] The land on which the icehouses stood was eventually donated to Falmouth for the building of a new school, aptly named Lawrence School (not to be confused with Lawrence Academy).

Sidney valued self-reliance, especially in his own children. His son Frederick V. Lawrence recounted, "As a kid, I used to love to ride my bicycle. One day down in Woods Hole village I fell off the bicycle. I sat on the roadside howling in pain. Sidney came along in his Dodge coupe, stopped the car, leaned out the window and looked at me. Then he drove off. This made me madder than hell to think he refused to show me some sympathy and help me. From that lesson, he taught me to 'look out for Freddie.'"[161]

In 1920, Sidney was elected to head the town highway surveyor department at the annual town meeting. According to his son, he was a tough boss, causing the town help to complain, so he lost the subsequent election. In true Woods Hole fashion, he bounced back, diving fully into his general contracting business and earning a large state road contract for Falmouth. Unfortunately, Sidney was a better builder than businessman, and he found himself taking on debt during the Depression, unable to turn things around. His son recalled that his father's "strength and perseverance only encouraged [my] determination to work for him and to help straighten out the family finances."[162] Sidney's "Yankee shrewdness," as Frederick Lawrence described it, was appreciated by his fellow citizens, earning him their admiration and trust. Despite his poor business skills, he was chosen to serve on the town's Finance Committee and the Planning Board and was also senior warden at the Church of the Messiah.

Things improved significantly once Frederick took the reins in 1933. Leveraging his father's fleet of heavy equipment, he formed a new company and began to work off the $100,000 of debt that Sidney had accumulated. The two men joined forces to grow the business, Sidney's experience complementing Frederick's college business courses, and the Frederick V. Lawrence Inc. company flourished. They went on to build the

*Right*: Portrait of Sidney Lawrence. *WHHM.*

*Below*: East End Meeting House in Hatchville, built in 1797 with endowment from the Lawrence family. *WHHM.*

stone pier at the Woods Hole Yacht Club during Edward Norman's tenure and garnered plenty of construction work when the Hurricane of 1938 crashed into Falmouth.

Josephine Lawrence was pleased to see Frederick succeed, having supported him through his academic struggles in childhood. She initially envisioned quite a different career path for her only son, however. As Frederick described, "Inspired by the Captain Lawrence who gave us the motto, 'Don't give up the ship,' it was decided by both my mother and her mother (even before I was born), that there should be another sea captain in the family. In anticipation, when I was born one of my ears was pierced and fitted with a gold ring, as this was the tradition for those bound for the open seas."[163] To that end, Lawrence was enrolled in the U.S. Naval Academy Preparatory School (NAPS) in Newport, Rhode Island, for two winters, but he failed to pass the Naval Academy entrance exam, dashing his mother's dreams. Instead, he graduated from Lawrence High School, followed by additional college prep at the Moses Brown Preparatory School in Providence, Rhode Island, and a successful academic career at the University of Maryland engineering school.

In 1951, after purchasing the Nickerson House, Sidney Lawrence received approval to convert the building into five apartments, and he removed the street-facing porch.[164] The apartments were rented primarily to members of the scientific community. No doubt some brilliant and accomplished minds spent summers in the various apartments, in addition to the aforementioned Nobel Prize winner, Dr. Otto Loewl.

Josephine died in 1962, followed by her husband in 1965. No surprise that both Sidney and Josephine are buried in Woods Hole Cemetery. When the family sold the house following Sidney Lawrence's death, they found an interested buyer within the village, starting the half-century tenure of the Roslanskys' stewardship of the house.

JOHN ROSLANSKY AND PRISCILLA Fenn met in Woods Hole in the summer of 1952 when they were lab partners at the Marine Biological Laboratory.[165] John grew up in Minnesota during the Great Depression, when frugality, resourcefulness and resiliency were critical to survival, so it is no wonder that he was drawn to Woods Hole. After graduating from Gustavus Adolphus College in 1948, he earned his master's degree at Oregon State University and went on to earn his doctorate from the University of California at Berkeley in 1956.

Priscilla, known as Pucky, grew up in Rochester, New York, and her curriculum vitae is beyond impressive. After graduating from Smith College in 1947, she earned her master's degree "as a member of the first class at Harvard Medical School to include women."[166] She went on to earn her doctorate in microbiology at the University of Rochester, teaching at Rutgers University and the University of Illinois and researching at the MBL during the summer.

John and Pucky married in 1953, settling first in Berkeley, California, and then spending several years in Copenhagen, where John completed a fellowship. They moved permanently to Woods Hole in 1963, and each made a mark on village life, Pucky as a civic activist and John as a real estate investor, scooping up multiple properties around town. In 1966, Pucky and John bought the Nickerson House from the Lawrence estate, and the family would own the property for over fifty years. With five (and later, six) apartments, the Millfield house was a revolving door of young students, doctoral candidates and probably a few Nobel laureates as well. John Roslansky served as editor in chief for the Nobel Conferences at his alma mater from 1965 to 1975 and likely lured some of these brilliant scientists to Woods Hole over the years.

The Roslanskys' youngest son, William, or Bill as he was known throughout the village, honed his home repair skills working on the house. The building was fifty years old when John and Pucky purchased it, and things were in need of attention. With five kitchens, six water heaters and six boilers, something was bound to fail every year. Bill recalls replacing shingles, patching walls and getting the front and back stairs up to code as a young man. He took his home repair skills to a new level when he became an architect. In 2017, Bill made his mark on the town as the project architect for renovating Pie in the Sky Bakery & Cafe, a favorite hangout for locals and visitors alike. Bill succeeded in creating a functional space that retains the character the coffee hotspot has developed since its founding in 1982.

Having grown up in the Midwest during the Depression, John was a waste-not, want-not kind of guy who could fix anything. Bill recalls helping his father update the small room located closest to Eel Pond, which served as the laundry room for more than half a century. Imagine today allocating space with an expansive waterfront view to the washroom—not likely. They suspected the room was insulated, but much to their surprise, when they removed the floorboards, they discovered it was insulated with dried seaweed. Wads and wads of seaweed were removed from under the laundry room and piled up along the seawall. Of course, they couldn't (or wouldn't) reuse that material, which was surely not up to code, but it was quick work to recycle it from whence it came…back over the seawall.

Pucky was active in community life, attending town meetings, joining the League of Women Voters, serving on the Falmouth Zoning Board of Appeals and volunteering with Falmouth Community Television, making an enormous and positive impact on the town aside from her scientific endeavors.

John died in 2003, and Pucky died in 2011. Both are buried in the cemetery next to the Church of the Messiah. Their children, several of whom still live in Woods Hole, continued to manage the house on Eel Pond as rental apartments until 2018, when they sold it to my husband and me.

And that brings the narrative of the house on Millfield to current day. Having looked back at its history, the unusual circumstances of its initial mortgage, the exterior changes over the years and the interesting people who lived within its walls, the house tells a fascinating story. The Nickerson House has been owned by a seafaring mailman, a millionaire, a venerable town elder and two brilliant scientists. The house promises many more years of welcoming fascinating people who are looking to soak up the Woods Hole atmosphere or contribute to its scholarship.

Beyond its history, old homes and the interesting people who lived (and still live) in the village, Woods Hole has much to offer the world in the years to come. It stands at the forefront of researching vital climate data and developing strategies to adapt to a changing universe while simultaneously hosting world-class athletic events and cultural performances. Having examined Woods Hole's past, it's time to delve into Woods Hole today and see where it is headed in the years ahead.

# BOOK IV
# THE FUTURE

———◆———

*Learn from yesterday, live for today, hope for tomorrow. The important thing is not to stop questioning. Curiosity has its own reason for existing.*
—*Albert Einstein*

*15*

# Cape Cod in a Nut (or Clam) Shell

F or many, Cape Cod represents quintessential New England, where Colonial houses, antique shops and tales of pirates and shipwrecks abound. And while the area is certainly steeped in history, European settlers who flocked to the region were modern thinkers in their day, adventurous pilgrims searching for religious tolerance and independence from an overbearing state system. Modernism can still be found on Cape Cod, from the exceptional twentieth-century houses in the Outer Cape to the cutting-edge scientific research happening in Woods Hole. Cape Cod's past and present lay the groundwork for a bright future, not just for the Cape, but for the world at large.

To the casual visitor, Cape Cod is one place, a sixty-five-mile-long hook of land replete with sandy beaches, golf courses and bike trails. Yet each of the Cape's fifteen towns is unique. Provincetown offers an offbeat artistic experience, while Sandwich lends a historic atmosphere and Dennis provides pristine beaches. Of course, Falmouth is the loveliest Cape Cod town, with its Main Street lined with specialty shops, shoreline walks and year-round activity.

Each town on the Cape contains smaller villages within its boundaries. Woods Hole is one such village within the town of Falmouth, which has eight villages in total: North Falmouth, East Falmouth, West Falmouth, Hatchville, Teaticket, Falmouth Village, Waquoit and Woods Hole. Geographically, the Cape is further organized into four distinct regions: Upper Cape, Mid

Cape, Lower Cape and Outer Cape. The easiest way to keep the regions straight is to envision the Cape as an arm, raised Rosie the Riveter style, off the southern coast of Massachusetts. Now imagine that arm is relaxed, dangling its fingers down, the tips of which would be Provincetown. The area at the top, made up of Bourne, Falmouth, Mashpee and Sandwich, is the Upper Cape. The stocky core section, including Barnstable, Dennis and Yarmouth, is considered Mid Cape, with Barnstable serving as the county seat for the entire Cape. The "elbow" includes Brewster, Chatham, Harwich and Orleans and is referred to as the Lower Cape. The Outer Cape includes the area that Bartholomew Gosnold first identified as Cape Cod in 1602: Eastham, Wellfleet, Truro and Provincetown.[167]

Well into the twentieth century, the roads leading to the tip of the peninsula were poor, and the Outer Cape maintained an aura of seclusion and wildness. For decades before the Mid-Cape Highway was constructed in 1926, artists and naturalists were drawn to the Outer Cape, spending May through October in rustic cottages, writing and painting, soaking up the views and studying the wildlife. The area was sparsely populated, and

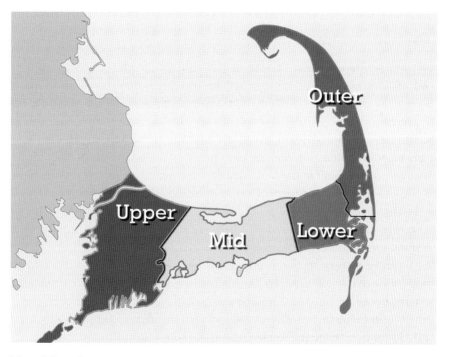

Map of Cape Cod regions created by John Stringfellow, a realtor, property developer and artist. www.capecodstar.com. *John Stringfellow.*

life among the dunes of Truro and Wellfleet offered a dramatic contrast to the congested conditions experienced in New York City or Boston. The area remained a favorite spot for the creative set, but after World War II, with the towns accessible by car and boat, the earlier solitude diminished.

Fearing the loss of pristine shoreline along the Atlantic coast of the Outer Cape, the National Park Service, in partnership with local residents and by an act of Congress, established the Cape Cod National Seashore in 1961. Encompassing sixty-eight square miles, the National Seashore management differs from other preservation efforts, balancing conservation with the demands of modern life. Development is strictly forbidden along nearly forty miles of shoreline, yet preservationists recognized that the economic well-being of the Outer Cape community was critical to its long-term survival and required a smart approach to much-needed development. This pragmatic attitude was championed decades earlier by the great conservationist and twenty-fifth president of the United States Theodore Roosevelt, who believed "conservation means development as much as it does protection. I recognize the right and duty of this generation to develop and use the natural resources of our land; but I do not recognize the right to waste them, or to rob, by wasteful use, the generations that come after us."[168] Roosevelt intended to harness present-day opportunities without destroying the country's future.

In an unprecedented move, Congress established a Citizens Advisory Committee, made up of local residents and officials, guiding the establishment and management of the new park. The result was public and private land adjacent to each other, benefiting from wise decisions made in the best interest of preserving the natural landscape of each. In 2007, the conservation effort was further expanded with the creation of the Cape Cod Modern House Trust, a grassroots organization that seeks to preserve the collection of "significant modern houses" built in the region during the mid-twentieth century by some of the nation's leading designers, many of which fell into despair.

Today, the Outer Cape is still known for its bohemian atmosphere, a haven for artists, surfers and naturalists. The ferry arrives in "P'town" from Boston in ninety minutes, and it feels like a world apart. The Lower Cape draws the beautiful people to the trendy shops and restaurants and offers family-friendly beaches and bike trails. Mid Cape is the center of commercial activity, home to big-box stores, ferries to the islands and the airport. One can also find charming villages and secluded beaches along the north coast and old-money "cottages" tucked along the south shore.

Until the seven-mile-long Cape Cod Canal was completed in 1914, the Cape was physically connected to mainland Massachusetts. The concept of building a canal first surfaced in 1623, proffered by Miles Standish of the nearby Plymouth Colony. The low-lying area, traversed by the Manomet and Scussett Rivers, seemed an ideal spot to divert ships away from the dangerous Cape Cod shoals. The artificial bifurcation made by the canal, finally completed three hundred years later, resulted in some strange geographic anomalies. For example, as one of the settlements that straddled the Manomet and Scussett riverbeds, the town of Bourne actually exists both on and off the Cape. Likewise, villages such as Onset (as in, the onset, or beginning, of Cape Cod) had enjoyed proximity to Cape Cod, welcoming summer visitors since the 1880s. Now, though only five miles from the Bourne Bridge, it is viewed as "off-Cape." Without the bridge traffic clogging the area, those in Onset may consider that a blessing.

Some old-timers still wax nostalgic about the drive to Cape Cod "back in the day." In his exquisitely descriptive book *The Big House*, George Colt recounts the sights, smells and emotions experienced during family trips to the Cape: "For many years, the highway ended seven miles from the Cape Cod Canal in a jumble of warning signs, flashing lights, and—lest anyone fail to heed these—a cement roadblock. Motorists were forced to detour onto Route 6, an old two-lane thoroughfare ambitiously known as the Cranberry Highway, which made its way to the Bourne Bridge through a gauntlet of motels, clam shacks, dairy bars, antique stores, trailer parks, and bait shops as garish and alluring as a carnival midway, offering a glimpse of what to my dazzled childhood eyes passed for sin: shopping, squalor, bad taste.…They were beloved milestones on our annual pilgrimage, as essential to our vision of Cape Cod as any lighthouse or sand dune. Indeed, throughout my youth I assumed that the highway had been deliberately designed to end prematurely so that every motorist could experience Route 6 as a sort of ecological transition zone between mainland and Cape."[169] George Colt continued to take this circuitous route to the bridge long after completion of the highway bypass, a reminder that while progress marches on, some experiences are worth preserving.

When visiting Cape Cod, it is nearly impossible to avoid the Upper Cape, home to Falmouth, Bourne, Sandwich and Mashpee, as both the Bourne and Sagamore Bridges reside there. Conversely, it's easy to drive right through, headed to the beaches of the Outer Cape or the golf courses in Hyannis. Some visitors know Falmouth—and by extension, Woods Hole—only as the terminus of the ferry that carries them across Vineyard Sound to Martha's Vineyard. But Woods Hole, as it has done since the whaling days, continues to evolve and grow, figuratively if not literally, ensuring its survival and relevance in today's fast-paced world.

*16*

# WHY WOODS HOLE MATTERS

## *The Future Is Now*

E ver since Bartholomew Gosnold sailed from England to explore the area in 1602, the sea has played a critical role in the successes—and failures—of Cape Cod's European settlers. The ocean was their highway, the transportation route that carried them to New England's shores. Having made the treacherous journey, early settlers were keenly aware of the ocean's danger as well as its bounty.

The Wampanoag people, Cape Cod's earliest settlers, relied on both the land and the ocean. The women cultivated maize, beans and squash (vital components for succotash, a diet staple) and supplemented this with fish caught by the men. When Europeans first arrived, they were unprepared for the rocky soil, harsh climate and unfamiliar garden pests. Many of the seeds they brought with them were ill-suited for the cold, sandy soil. They struggled with fishing, as few of them were trained fishermen, and their fishing hooks were the wrong size to catch the local fish.[170]

The settlers learned from their Native neighbors how to survive in this new environment, before the relationship of cooperation turned to one of conflict. Both farming and fishing skills improved, and the sea became a critical partner in the commercial success of the settlers. Nineteenth-century Cape Cod was home to master shipbuilders and experienced sea captains. Whaling and commercial trade flourished, and in Woods Hole, fertilizer was produced from seabird guano mixed with local fish. Products and skills developed in Woods Hole affected commerce throughout the country.

In the twenty-first century, the tiny village in the southwest corner of Cape Cod continues to adapt to the changing times. With a population of 850, Woods Hole punches above its weight, and four examples (though there are many) illustrate how the community is moving forward, year after year attracting the best talent in academia, athletics and the arts.

Many people are aware of the submersible technology that led to the discovery of the *Titanic*, but do they recall that WHOI innovations created that technology? The Falmouth Road Race, founded by a local bartender, with ninety-two runners in its first year, is now a bucket-list item for any serious runner. The creative community is discovering the unique offerings at the Woods Hole Film Festival. And perhaps most critically, communities around the world benefit from groundbreaking research and recommendations coming out of Woods Hole on climate concerns. Resilient Woods Hole is a private-public collaboration of scientists, administrators and business leaders, working together on climate issues at the highest level and ensuring Woods Hole remains cutting-edge, functional and exceptional. The sea is an important component of each of these initiatives, contributing positively—and occasionally negatively—but always integral to the overall experience.

# To the Bottom of the Deep (Navy) Blue Sea

The U.S. Navy recognized early the value of Cape Cod to its mission, first as a strategic asset between Boston and New York and then as a fertile environment for scientific research to enhance its military capability. The navy's relationship with the scientific community in Woods Hole is as old as the community itself, and discoveries made there resulted in more resilient ships, advanced sonar capabilities and improved mapping of the ocean floor. These advancements were crucial to the military as it waged war against the German fleet of U-boats during both the First and Second World Wars.

Throughout World War II, WHOI scientists focused on elements of the marine environment that were critical to naval warfare. They studied the effects of underwater explosives, identified paint that could minimize "marine fouling"—when marine life attaches itself to the hull of a ship, thus slowing it down—and researched the ways in which ocean salinity affects sonic efficiency. At the end of the war, the physical presence of the U.S. Navy quickly waned in Woods Hole, but its partnership with the Woods Hole Oceanographic Institution did not.

During the Cold War, the government focused on acoustics and countering perceived threats of Soviet submarines. In 1950, the National Science Foundation (NSF) was formed, gradually taking the funding lead on these vital research projects. Today, the navy remains focused on ship-based ocean study in the form of research vessels and submersibles. The current fleet of vessels working out of Woods Hole include the R/V *Neil Armstrong* and R/V *Atlantis*, owned by the Office of Naval Research and operated by WHOI.

In the 1960s, this partnership in advanced ocean research reached new depths with the launch of DSV *Alvin*, the first U.S. research submersible. Commissioned in 1964, this tiny submersible could dive to six thousand feet while carrying two passengers. Named to honor Allyn Vine, a WHOI engineer and biophysicist who championed its development, *Alvin* truly went where no man had gone before. Since then, *Alvin* has received a continual stream of upgrades so that, half a century after its launch, it is still in service. Apart from its name and a few random parts, however, every bit of the original submersible has been upgraded or replaced.[171]

*Alvin*'s conquests are as varied as the marine features it studies. Its first major mission was in 1966, when a U.S. Air Force B-52 bomber collided midair with a refueling tanker over Spain. The disintegrating plane dropped four hydrogen bombs, three of which were recovered in fields along the coast. The fourth bomb tumbled into the Mediterranean Sea, its exact location unknown. After two months of painstaking exploration, *Alvin* located the bomb on the seafloor. In the course of the search, the crew honed its operating skills and pushed the boundaries of *Alvin*'s capabilities.

Over the next decade, *Alvin* was instrumental in some of the most profound oceanic discoveries of the twentieth century, including confirming the existence of hydrothermal systems on the seafloor, which sustain life at great depths by providing energy from the earth (chemosynthesis) rather than energy from the sun (photosynthesis). *Alvin* continues to aid marine scientists as they explore life on the ocean floor in ever more remote and challenging locations.

In 1975, Woods Hole, or at least its scientific community, made a splash into pop culture with the release of the movie *Jaws*, based on Peter Benchley's best-selling book. Matt Hooper, played by Richard Dreyfuss, is sent to the beleaguered (and fictional) Amity Island by the generic "oceanographic institute on the mainland," a clear reference to WHOI, and he shares his knowledge of all things shark—*Carcharodon carcharias*, as he prefers—with the islanders. While the movie certainly did not endear the shark community to

*Alvin*, Woods Hole Oceanographic Institution's premier submersible, as it looked in 1966. *Digital Commonwealth*.

the common beachgoer, it inspired a new generation of marine biologists and oceanographers.

In 1985, Woods Hole made headlines when Robert Ballard, retired navy officer and professor at WHOI, successfully located the wreck of the RMS *Titanic*, the "unsinkable" luxury ocean liner that sank in 12,500 feet of water in the frigid North Atlantic Ocean in April 1912. As with Ballard's earlier (and arguably more important) discovery of hydrothermal vents near the Galapagos Islands, this was a joint venture with the navy. He used new technology in his search for the *Titanic* while conducting a secret U.S. military effort to locate the wreckage of two nuclear-powered submarines that sank in the area two decades earlier. The U.S. Navy was desperate to reclaim the vessels, which carried a treasure trove of military technology, without alerting the Soviets. Ballard's mission provided the perfect cover.

Ballard's crew located the two submarines and, aided by the state-of-the-art deep-sea robot *Argo*, observed that the currents carried matter from the sinking submarines much farther than anticipated, creating a larger debris field. Ballard applied this lesson to his search methods, focusing on locating the debris field of the *Titanic*, rather than trying to spot the much smaller hull of the ship, allowing his team to cover more territory in less time. Within two weeks, he located the *Titanic* on the seafloor. The discovery made headlines around the world.

Ballard returned to the site in July 1986 to further document the wreckage, using *Alvin* to complete a thorough study. Subsequent documentaries introduced the scientifically curious to the amazing feats of submersible vessels, which represent a 150-year collaboration between the U.S. Navy and the scientists of Woods Hole. With over 90 percent of the ocean floor still unmapped, Woods Hole's ocean experts have much more to contribute to our knowledge of the planet in the future.

# Falmouth Road Race

In 1972, the Summer Olympic Games were held in Munich, the first time the Summer Games were held in Germany since the infamous 1936 Olympics held under the Nazi regime. The 1972 Games were overshadowed by the deaths of eleven Israeli athletes and coaches in the "Munich massacre," a botched hostage situation orchestrated by Palestinian terrorists.

Following the tragedy, the Games were suspended for several hours, but the International Olympic Committee declared that the "Games must go on," and following a memorial ceremony in the Olympic Stadium, they resumed. The Men's Marathon was held on September 10, five days after the massacre, and for the first time since Johnny Hayes's victory in 1908, the event was won by an American. The victorious runner, Frank Shorter, was born in Munich, the son of a U.S. Army physician. But no question, Frank was all American.

Four thousand miles away, Tommy Leonard was tending bar at Brothers 4 in Falmouth Heights. A running fanatic before that was really a thing, Leonard was glued to the TV, offering commentary on the race, and legend has it he refused to pour a drink until Frank Shorter crossed the finish line. Since the race was over by 11:12 a.m. local time, it may not have been a huge issue. Frank Shorter's victory sparked a running craze, and Tommy Leonard headed the pack.

During the off-season, Leonard worked at the Eliot Lounge in Boston, its walls covered with photos of the great runners of the day: Joan Benoit, Frank Shorter, Lynn Jennings and Craig Virgin, to name a few. Leonard developed

The famous Falmouth Road Race as it rounds Nobska Point at the One Mile Marker, draws over ten thousand runners to Woods Hole every August. *From the* New York Sun.

an audacious plan for a race from the Captain Kidd Restaurant in Woods Hole to the Brothers 4…*and to invite Frank Shorter to run the race*![172]

August 15, 1973, Tommy Leonard's thirty-ninth birthday, marked the inaugural Falmouth "marathon," an unconventional seven-mile slog through the rain on a day so miserable, the ninety-two runners took shelter inside the Captain Kidd prior to the start to keep warm. Proceeds were donated to the high school girls track team, and an iconic Cape Cod tradition was born.

Two years later, in 1975, Frank Shorter fulfilled Tommy's vision by running in Falmouth, starting an annual rivalry with Boston Marathon legend Bill Rodgers, as they took home five Falmouth Road Race victories between them. Over the years, all the Boston greats ran the Falmouth Road Race, including Joan Benoit, Alberto Salazar, Jenny Tuthill and Lynn Jennings.

The racecourse hugs the shore and passes the Nobska Lighthouse, with sweeping views of Vineyard Sound, before heading inland, offering shade along with hills. Up next is a two-mile stretch along Shore Drive, which is blissfully flat but offers no shade and can be absolutely grueling on a sunny day. At Mile 5, the course enters town and skirts around Falmouth Harbor, and then it gets really tough. The final half mile involves a seemingly never-ending hill. After "cresting" for the third time, the runner is finally rewarded with a long downhill sweep to the finish line.

Each mile of this wonderful, excruciating race is punctuated with four-foot-high mile markers painted permanently on the road. For those unable to secure a spot for the official Falmouth Road Race, they can experience the joy—and agony—of running the iconic course on the other 364 days of the year.

Today, the Falmouth Road Race is a bucket list item for any road race fanatic. The field has grown to over ten thousand participants and draws runners from around the world. Consistently listed as one of the most iconic races in the country, after fifty years, enthusiasm for the annual contest, with its quirky distance, grueling hills and joyous spectators, has not waned. It takes a herculean effort, thousands of volunteers and some big-name sponsors to run a race of this magnitude. As with many things in Falmouth, it takes sheer grit and determination to get the race—and runners—across the finish line.

# THE WOODS HOLE FILM FESTIVAL

For more than thirty years, independent filmmakers have gathered in Falmouth to share their cinematic visions at the Woods Hole Film Festival (WHFF). Founded in 1991 by Judy Laster and Katy Davis, both children of Woods Hole scientists, the festival has grown from a one-day event featuring 5 films to an eight-day event featuring approximately 150 films, selected from nearly 1,000 films submitted from around the world.[173] The WHFF focuses on the works of emerging filmmakers from across the country and also filmmakers of varied experience from New England and now includes international entries. There is a special emphasis on films with Cape Cod links or that highlight issues relevant to the quality of life on Cape Cod.

The festival takes place the last Saturday in July through the first Saturday in August, and the venues range from the Clapp Auditorium at WHOI to locations at Falmouth Academy, a far cry from the screenings in the early years that were held in the Old Woods Hole Fire Station. The offerings beyond screening films have also grown, with evening entertainment at local restaurants, panel discussions and workshops on a variety of relevant topics.

Festival organizers work year-round to create a vibrant and welcoming event and recently have doubled down on a commitment to highlight the special relationships unique to Woods Hole, namely the proximity and accessibility of the marine scientists and their projects. To that end, the WHFF recently launched the Film & Science Initiative, connecting filmmakers and scientists in an effort to increase public understanding of science. "The emphasis on films that amplify science is reflected in the marine imagery on the film festival's posters, which in recent years have come to feature an octopus."[174]

In 2020, the Woods Hole Film Festival was at a crossroads. Like so many organizations, the WHFF faced Covid-19 pandemic closures, and a way forward seemed elusive. In the spirit of their Yankee forebears, the leadership figured out how to make lemonade out of lemons, shifting the entire festival on its head. The film festival opened as a virtual event during its scheduled week, July 25–August 1, 2020,

The Woods Hole Film Festival logo is constantly evolving, but the octopus element seems to be a fan favorite. *Woods Hole Film Festival.*

with 188 films, 42 of them feature-length documentaries or narratives, and 146 short films, available to "participants" online. The team also managed to reimagine the panel discussions, workshops and other activities, critical to connecting participants and traditionally experienced in person, but now presented online.

This experimental gathering of the Woods Hole Film Festival was transformative. No longer constrained by the limited participation space in Woods Hole, the festival suddenly was accessible to interested parties from much farther afield. It encouraged a broad range of participation and allowed ticket holders the flexibility to watch as many films as they wished, with a greater degree of convenience. The following year, the in-person film festival returned to Woods Hole but with the virtual program baked into the event. Though participants were encouraged to attend the virtual events in "real time" in order to fully participate in the live discussions, the revised format allowed them to go back and see other films that aired concurrently. For the first time ever, it was possible—with a significant time commitment— to view all the offerings of the film festival.

All this speaks to the fortitude and resilience one comes to expect in Woods Hole. Despite its money and celebrity, the Telluride Film Festival was canceled in 2020, as was Cannes. By 2021, both groups had figured out how to accomplish what the WHFF had mastered a year earlier. That same year, the Woods Hole Film Festival released the short documentary *Bruce and Alvin*, which was developed under the auspices of the Film & Science Initiative as a co-production with Oscar-nominated filmmaker Josh Seftel, founder of SmartyPants, Brooklyn. The film tells the story of the ever-evolving submersible *Alvin* and Bruce Strickrott, its chief pilot. This initiative serves to amplify the research and discoveries within the Woods Hole scientific community, broadcasting knowledge far beyond the scope of the village itself. The Woods Hole Film Festival is an exciting example of a small community coming together with resilience and intellectual curiosity to bring understanding and enlightenment to the world at large.

# RESILIENT WOODS HOLE

Today, ocean conditions are taking center stage in environmental discussions around the world. Historically, the ocean's proximity in coastal communities was met with awe and some trepidation. Houses were set back from the shore, leaving the coastline itself as a buffer zone. Since the mid-nineteenth century, however, appreciation for ocean views and fresh breezes off the water led to a building boom along the coast, with grand homes popping up on cliffs overlooking the sea and cottages dotting sand bars, such as those lost at Napatree, Rhode Island, in the Hurricane of 1938. Exposure to the elements put these homes at greater risk during weather events than homes built further inland, yet a desire and determination to "conquer the sea" prevailed.

Environmental conversations are focused on the effects of climate change on coastal communities. The topic has been toxically politicized, but there is little dispute that coastal communities are vulnerable to high winds, flooding and other hazards, especially as more homes are built closer to the water's edge. Independent of any climate discussions, many coastal areas are dynamic, changing constantly, as powerful waves pull sand away from the coastline in some areas while piling it up in other spots. The shoreline of Cape Cod looks quite different today than when Bartholomew Gosnold first arrived, and that change is chronic. A community's ability to protect itself from atmospheric events (hurricanes, sea-level changes, beach erosion) is critical to its long-term survival, and the scientists in Woods Hole are at ground zero, both geographically and vocationally.

Many WHOI and MBL buildings are at sea level, no more than a few dozen feet from Vineyard Sound. When storms hit, especially when they peak during high tide, the effects are felt throughout the village. The MBL docks in Eel Pond become submerged, waves crash over the seawall at Waterfront Park and frequently the lower levels of academic buildings are flooded. These scenarios are nothing new, but the risk of extensive damage to the buildings and equipment is gravely concerning, as is the threat of flooding tides to homes and wetlands in the village's low-lying areas.

There is no collection of institutions better equipped to assess the risk and resolutions of current climate issues than those in Woods Hole. Flooding is a real issue that has affected village inhabitants for centuries, and it is unquestionably in everyone's best interest to understand the environmental issues better. WHOI has been collecting data from coastal communities for decades, and focuses, in partnership with the National Science Foundation and the Office of Naval Research, on changing conditions in the Arctic Ocean. Its innovative approach to Polar Science places WHOI at the forefront of one of the critical public policy discussions of our time.

In 2020, three of Woods Hole's major science institutions—WHOI, MBL and NOAA—formed an innovative collaboration aptly named Resilient Woods Hole. The tagline of the group is "Private-public investment to ensure the future of a seaside community and blue economy village."[175] They partnered with local stakeholders from business, residential and other science communities in Woods Hole to leverage their "intellectual horsepower and management skills," pooling their resources to undertake advanced research on the impacts of "sea-level rise, coastal flooding, shoreline loss, and associated challenges."[176] Working with government and private sector grants and using current and historic data collected by the core institutions, the group created likely flooding scenarios, sharing findings with the local community through a series of symposiums and conducting seminars to encourage input for solutions. This consortium manages to avoid the "blame" trap, leaving that to others, instead reviewing the empirical evidence and looking for solutions.

Resilient Woods Hole and its collection of homeowners, scientists, businesspeople and artists are motivated by their commitment to remain in Woods Hole, connected to the sea, not running off to higher ground. Access to the water is critical to research at all the Woods Hole institutions, and it inspires artists, residents and businesses alike. Anchored by the blue economy, the community aims to protect its relationship to the sea while learning how best to live with the changing conditions. The project is certainly unique, as here, the doctor is also the patient; researchers are looking for solutions that will affect them directly. Woods Hole is poised to be the petri dish for solutions that can guide other coastal communities, making Woods Hole not only resilient but also exceptionally relevant now and in the future.

THESE FOUR EXAMPLES ARE just some of the creative and smart ways Woods Hole has tethered its inherent fortitude to an ever-changing environment, whether physical, economic or cultural. Some communities insist on growth to maintain viability, which can result in bulldozing the past and losing connection to important historical lessons. In Woods Hole, the past is present up and down Water Street, in the Candle House building that once housed spermaceti manufacturing and at the Landfall Restaurant, built with scraps of lumber and remnants of days past. And yet the village of Woods Hole continues to move forward, to a future that its scientists will influence in ways we cannot yet imagine, driven by resourcefulness, grit and a deep love of community.

*17*

# WHY HISTORIC PRESERVATION MATTERS

## *Improving Our Future by Preserving Our Past*

istoric preservation projects can be lofty or humble. The need to protect and restore important buildings, such as Thomas Jefferson's Monticello and Rome's Colosseum, is self-evident. It is also worthwhile to safeguard places that contribute to the distinctive heritage and culture of a particular community. The Texas State Fair, the Garden District of New Orleans and Pike Place Market in Seattle offer a few examples. Sadly, the essence of our less famous communities is being lost to careless gentrification and aggressive modernization.

To appreciate the importance of historic preservation, one should understand the forces behind the preservation movement, consider its ecological benefits and contemplate the stories that are lost when heritage buildings and objects disappear.

FORMAL EFFORTS TO PROTECT America's past began with the founding of the Mount Vernon Ladies' Association, established in 1853, to maintain and operate the Mount Vernon estates, originally owned by President George Washington's family. The mansion had fallen into disrepair, rescued just in time by the patriotic fervor of a determined group of women, under the leadership of Ann P. Cunningham. In her twenty years at the helm, she created a nationwide framework of women to raise funds and manage the restoration team, working "with men, not around them."[177] The MVLA set a high bar for preservation standards and continues that mission today.

The historic preservation movement picked up steam in the early twentieth century, as older buildings, particularly within cities, were razed to make way for expanded road systems. Development threatened to erase many important sites, and not just buildings but also battlefields and small towns with distinctive architecture that defined their communities. For those who have visited Oak Bluffs on Martha's Vineyard, imagine if the gingerbread houses were razed and replaced with tall concrete hotels that were popularized in the 1920s.

As modern architecture swept the nation, many worried about the homogenization of America, especially in New England, with its distinctive culture and buildings dating to the seventeenth century. The Society for the Preservation of New England Antiquities (now called Historic New England) was established in 1910, the oldest regional preservation society in the country. The group collected a myriad of items particular to New England's history, preserving fine furniture and mundane objects of everyday life, such as spinning wheels and cooking utensils.

The U.S. National Trust for Historic Preservation[178] was founded in 1949, but it took several dramatic development projects in the 1960s to set off alarm bells and put the preservation movement into high gear. One such project was the demolition of Penn Station in New York City. Built in 1910, this railway hub was considered a masterpiece of the Beaux-Arts style. When train travel declined after World War II, the station was sold and demolished in 1963 to make way for Madison Square Garden. Its destruction was emblematic of the damage wrought by rapid economic growth and development, along with a dearth of urban planning. Its demise led to the creation of New York's Landmark Preservation Commission in 1965. Thankfully, preservation efforts by this commission in 1967 protected Grand Central Station from a similar fate.

Washington, D.C., was also experiencing a battle between preservation and modernization. When First Lady Jacqueline Kennedy moved into the White House in 1961, she encountered a hodgepodge of furnishings and design. President Truman's extensive renovation (1948–52) ensured that the building was updated and the foundation sound, but little effort had gone into furnishing the Executive Mansion. Mrs. Kennedy envisioned a White House full of antiques, furnished in the style of its past residents. As she told Hugh Sidey of *Life* magazine in a 1961 interview, "Everything in the White House must have a reason for being there. It would be a sacrilege merely to 'redecorate' it—a word I hate. It must be restored—and that has nothing to do with decoration. That is a question of scholarship."[179] To avoid the politically fraught task of asking Congress for public funds for her project, Kennedy established the White House Historical Association, soliciting donations from her wealthy and well-connected friends. The association raised additional funds by publishing the first official White House guidebook, *The White House: An Historic Guide*, now in its twenty-sixth edition. Since 1981, the association also creates and sells the annual Official White House Christmas Ornament, which sequentially honors past presidents and historical events and supports "the mission to enhance the understanding and appreciation of the Executive Mansion."[180]

But Kennedy's focus went beyond the White House. For several years prior to her husband's election, Congress had been looking to raze the residential buildings around Lafayette Square, directly across from the White House, in order to build high-rise government office buildings. The National Trust for Historic Preservation, housed in Decatur House on Lafayette Square, objected to the project, which would demolish what is now the Renwick Gallery, several historic townhomes and the Old Executive Office Building, destroying the sense of neighborhood Lafayette Square enjoyed. Though the plans were well underway, and President Kennedy had even given formal approval in 1961, Mrs. Kennedy pushed back, using her charm and connections to convince the planning committee to refine the plans and maintain Lafayette Square's character. Today, the White House Historical Association is headquartered in Decatur House, managing the property for the National Trust, and Lafayette Square retains its neighborhood essence.

Preservation efforts took a step backward in New York, however, when Grand Central's landmark designation was vacated by the courts in 1975, leaving it vulnerable to redevelopment. It was Jackie Kennedy, by now Mrs. Onassis, who helped rescue it a second time, imploring New York's Mayor Abraham Beame in a handwritten letter, "Is it not cruel to let our city die by degrees, stripped of all her proud moments, until there is nothing left of all her history and beauty to inspire our children? If they are not inspired by the past of our city, where will they find the strength to fight for her future?"[181] Next time you walk beneath the vaulted ceiling in Grand Central Station, please thank Jacqueline Kennedy Onassis.

*To preserve: (verb) to maintain something in its original or existing state. To keep something as it is, especially in order to prevent it from decaying or being damaged or destroyed.*

Preservation is at the core of human survival. Just as we should care for the environment for future generations, we also need to protect the physical reminders of our history. Yet the benefits of historic preservation go far beyond academic research, museums, and history classes; preservation brings with it environmental benefits and economic sustainability, which are often overlooked or misunderstood in the urban planning process.

Despite preservation efforts, it is commonplace to tear down older structures, replacing them with larger, updated buildings. Occasionally an effort is made to salvage remnants from older buildings, such as wood floor planks or decorative molding, but the majority of demolished homes end up in landfills. As with so many things, most notably clothing and furniture, ours has become a disposable society, far from the waste-not want-not mindset of previous generations, when dresses would be remade from one season to the next and eventually handed down or sewn into quilts. Furniture and appliances were refurbished, not replaced, when they simply needed a new part or a quick repair.

The same held true for buildings. A century ago, it was not uncommon that a house would be relocated when widening a road or expanding infrastructure. In Woods Hole, there are many such examples. WHOI's Discovery Center at 15 School Street, a "wood framed white church building was originally located on the south side of Water Street…and was moved to this location in 1949."[182] Likewise, the Shiverick House at 11 School Street was relocated when its original site was converted to a parking lot. It "was bought by Sidney Lawrence and moved around the corner to School Street in March of 1949."[183] Across the street is the Donaldson House, built in 1767 near Quisett. It was moved to School Street between 1848 and 1858 through fields or by water, as no road existed there at the time. Even the porch removed from the Nickerson House was repurposed at the Lawrences' home down the street.

A most astonishing example of preserving an old building comes from Cuttyhunk Island. When its Coast Guard station shut down, the building was moved intact to Menemsha on Martha's Vineyard. It was, and remains, a substantial building, with three full floors and a large cupola that served as a lookout. Built in 1937, it was still fairly new when Cuttyhunk Station was decommissioned in 1952, so the resourceful New Englanders floated the building across Vineyard Sound, pulled along by a barge. According to Diana Handy Goodhue, "It was rigged with explosives in case it capsized and became a navigation hazard."[184]

IN FAIRHAVEN, MASSACHUSETTS, TEN miles across Buzzards Bay from Woods Hole, Henry Rogers had the kind of money that could rebuild a town. Coming from modest beginnings, Rogers was determined to succeed, working as a delivery boy, then a railroad baggage handler, advancing to brakeman. He invested his earnings wisely, entering the oil industry in 1861, and by 1890 he was a vice president at Standard Oil Company and a very wealthy man. When he decided to bestow his largesse on Fairhaven, he quite literally reinvented the town, replacing all the schools, building a grand public library in his daughter's memory and planning a new—and quite large—town hall in the center of Fairhaven. Unfortunately, the spot he proposed for the town hall was already occupied, with three existing homes and lots of established trees.

In today's world, it is doubtful that such a situation would even slow down the development of the project. The houses would be razed and the lot would be clear-cut so that progress could continue without delay. But Rogers and his wife viewed things differently. One house had "to be demolished because moving it would require destroying desirable shade trees," so it was sold to a local farmer, who took it apart and recycled all "the woodwork and windows to build poultry houses."[185] Roger's wife, Abbie Rogers, purchased the second house, had it moved to a corner of the property and then deeded it back to the original owner. The third house was taken through eminent domain at twice its value and subsequently moved. Even on a project with a massive budget, destroying or discarding viable buildings (and trees) was unthinkable.

In the twenty-first century, too many urban planners assume replacing older buildings with new, efficient ones is a net positive for the environment. And though engineering advancements have increased energy efficiency in recent years, so-called green buildings, using LEED ratings to measure energy use and waste, are not always better. What is missing from the conversation is the reality that "the greenest building…is the one that is already built."[186] Carl Elefante articulated this idea in 2007, pointing out the obvious, that the energy, materials and financial support required to build a new building, and the waste created by destroying an old one, undermine the ecological and economic argument for teardowns. Jacqueline Kennedy understood this simple idea, which she shared with her preservation colleague David Finley in 1962. "Everyone wants to raze things & build efficient new buildings—[General Services administrator] Bernard Boutin is a preservationist & also he says it will be cheaper! Who else would ever have said that! None of those naughty showoff architects!"[187]

Clients are often told it is cheaper to build new than to restore, defying logic. The National Trust for Historic Preservation has set out to quantify the value of repurposing older buildings. It created Preservation Green Lab to investigate "the climate change reductions that might be offered by reusing and retrofitting existing buildings rather than demolishing and replacing them with new construction."[188] Its comprehensive research report concluded that "it can take between 10 and 80 years for a new, energy-efficient building to overcome…the negative climate change impacts that were created during the construction process."[189] More recently, studies are suggesting that new construction buildings are not reaching the seventy-five-year life span originally promoted, especially as inferior building materials and new-growth wood replace the more durable construction materials of the past. Additional research done in partnership with the Urban Land Institute draws similar conclusions.

The challenge is that renovating an older building requires creative thinking, broad knowledge of engineering and patience. There is no one-size-fits-all blueprint to repurpose Baltimore rowhouses or Craftsman bungalows. However, there is much to be learned and shared between similar projects, and the end result can positively reshape a community. The report sums up its findings: "The Bottom Line: Reusing existing buildings is good for the economy, the community and the environment. At a time when our country's foreclosure and unemployment rates remain high, communities would be wise to reinvest in their existing building stock. Historic rehabilitation has a thirty-two year track record of creating 2 million jobs and generating $90 billion in private investment. Studies show residential rehabilitation creates 50% more jobs than new construction."[190]

THE NATIONAL TRUST FOR Historic Preservation suggests that "historic preservation is a conversation with our past about our future."[191] Preservation is more than just saving old things; it actually is about storytelling. The stories that emerge from the study of people, their homes and their belongings illuminate not only what happened but also *why* it happened. Preserving the physical remnants of the past contributes to the scholarship and also helps us imagine what it was like to be in a particular place at a particular time. Tangible objects cannot tell the whole story, but they can offer a glimpse of another era in a way that a book cannot.

Millfield Street houses on the north shore of Eel Pond, Nickerson house second from left. *WHHM.*

Researching the house on Eel Pond uncovered a plethora of serendipitous relationships that connected us to the house and the village in unexpected ways. That Helen Sheehy's friend Mary Ramsbottom was related to the original owners of the house, for example, put my investigative skills into overdrive and led to additional discoveries and family stories, some accurate and others apocryphal. The house was an ordinary—albeit older—house, and there was no expectation that it held so many interesting and intertwined stories. The unexpected connections between past and present, links to our stomping grounds in Washington, D.C., and discovering friends' relationships with Falmouth added texture and depth to the story. And yet, why should this be so surprising? Everyone's life has interesting elements, moments that are funny, or tragic, or poignant. In one hundred years, what are those elements in your own life that others might find entertaining?

These discoveries underscore that every house and every family have stories to tell if one looks and listens. In this instance, the family is not mine, but the floors we walk on today in Woods Hole are the very same ones trod on a century ago by Walter and Helena. The awe I feel looking at the beautifully carved fireplace mantels throughout the house likely mirrors the pride the Nickersons felt gazing on the same. My family is now connected to the house and its history, and we feel obliged to protect the legacy of those who built and cared for it all these years.

An important theme emerged while writing this book, namely, a reminder that history marches on and that yesterday's current event becomes tomorrow's historical saga. What today we consider new and ordinary in fifty years will take on a different aura of relevance. Not all structures will be considered valuable, but buildings that are constructed with integrity and thoughtful style will deserve the protections we apply to notable older homes today.

The town of Falmouth (of which Woods Hole is a part) has fully embraced preservation, creating its Historic Preservation Plan in 2014. Recognizing the ongoing and inevitable development that coastal communities experience, Falmouth is dedicated to smart growth management, balancing economic needs and preservation best practices. It is not easy, as the town struggles with housing shortages, stormwater concerns and budget shortfalls, but Falmouth is working hard to leverage the state's Community Preservation Act to find solutions while protecting the essential character of the community and safeguarding its future.

In addition to protecting its heritage buildings, the various local Falmouth museums collect and archive letters, photographs and even small boats from its residents. Along with the exquisitely managed archives of the *Falmouth Enterprise*, these records were vital to uncovering the story of Nickerson family. Without them, and with so few descendants to keep the Nickerson family history alive, there might have been no clues to follow, and the history of the house would be lost. Instead, robust historic preservation provided a wealth of information not just about the Nickersons but about life on Eel Pond in centuries past. The stories we tell about the past create memories and a bond in the present, motivating us to protect that narrative for future generations. Starting with an ordinary house in a tiny village, that narrative can tell the history of a nation.

# APPENDIX

F amily Trees of the Nickerson and Nugent families: The tree headed by the parents of Walter E. Nickerson includes four generations, while the tree headed by the parents of Helena C. Nickerson includes three generations.

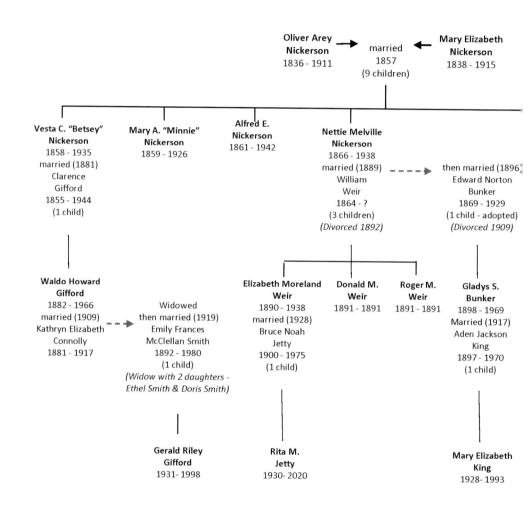

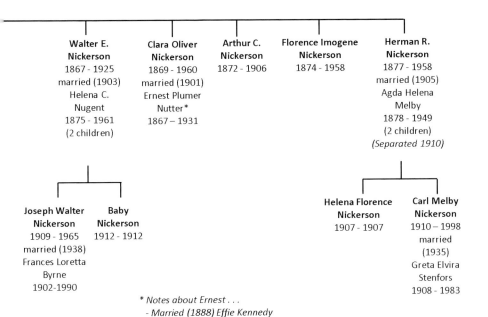

# NICKERSON FAMILY TREE

**Walter E. Nickerson**
1867 - 1925
married (1903)
Helena C. Nugent
1875 - 1961
(2 children)

**Clara Oliver Nickerson**
1869 - 1960
married (1901)
Ernest Plumer Nutter*
1867 – 1931

**Arthur C. Nickerson**
1872 - 1906

**Florence Imogene Nickerson**
1874 - 1958

**Herman R. Nickerson**
1877 - 1958
married (1905)
Agda Helena Melby
1878 - 1949
(2 children)
*(Separated 1910)*

**Joseph Walter Nickerson**
1909 - 1965
married (1938)
Frances Loretta Byrne
1902-1990

**Baby Nickerson**
1912 - 1912

**Helena Florence Nickerson**
1907 - 1907

**Carl Melby Nickerson**
1910 – 1998
married (1935)
Greta Elvira Stenfors
1908 - 1983

*\* Notes about Ernest . . .*
  *- Married (1888) Effie Kennedy*
    *Widowed 1890*
  *- Married (1891) Nellie Atwood*
    *(1 daughter – Ruth Plumer)*
    *Divorced by 1900*
  *-  Abandoned Clara in 1917*
  *-  Common Law Wife (1917 – 1931) Grace Loveland*

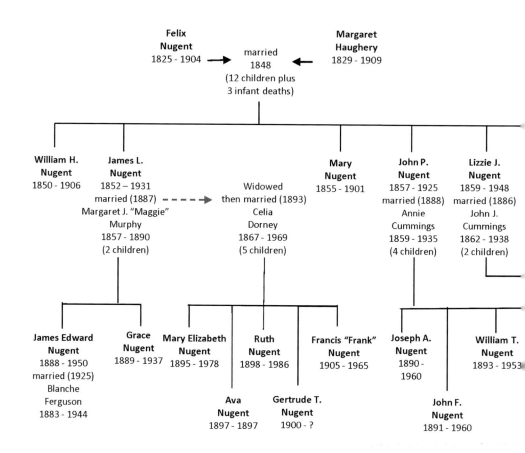

Felix
Nugent
1825 - 1904 → married
1848
(12 children plus
3 infant deaths) ← Margaret
Haughery
1829 - 1909

William H.
Nugent
1850 - 1906

James L.
Nugent
1852 – 1931
married (1887)
Margaret J. "Maggie"
Murphy
1857 - 1890
(2 children) - - - → Widowed
then married (1893)
Celia
Dorney
1867 - 1969
(5 children)

Mary
Nugent
1855 - 1901

John P.
Nugent
1857 - 1925
married (1888)
Annie
Cummings
1859 - 1935
(4 children)

Lizzie J.
Nugent
1859 - 1948
married (1886)
John J.
Cummings
1862 - 1938
(2 children)

James Edward
Nugent
1888 - 1950
married (1925)
Blanche
Ferguson
1883 - 1944

Grace
Nugent
1889 - 1937

Mary Elizabeth
Nugent
1895 - 1978

Ava
Nugent
1897 - 1897

Ruth
Nugent
1898 - 1986

Gertrude T.
Nugent
1900 - ?

Francis "Frank"
Nugent
1905 - 1965

Joseph A.
Nugent
1890 -
1960

John F.
Nugent
1891 - 1960

William T.
Nugent
1893 - 1953

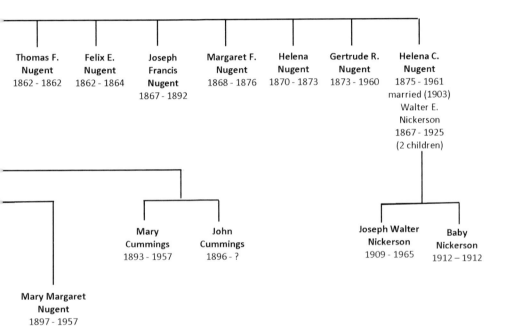

# NUGENT FAMILY TREE

**Thomas F. Nugent**
1862 - 1862

**Felix E. Nugent**
1862 - 1864

**Joseph Francis Nugent**
1867 - 1892

**Margaret F. Nugent**
1868 - 1876

**Helena Nugent**
1870 - 1873

**Gertrude R. Nugent**
1873 - 1960

**Helena C. Nugent**
1875 - 1961
married (1903)
Walter E. Nickerson
1867 - 1925
(2 children)

**Mary Cummings**
1893 - 1957

**John Cummings**
1896 - ?

**Joseph Walter Nickerson**
1909 - 1965

**Baby Nickerson**
1912 – 1912

**Mary Margaret Nugent**
1897 - 1957

# Notes

## Preface

1. After five years of research, Mary's daughter, Sara, shared a family album containing a number of enlightening pictures and documents.

## Chapter 1. How It All Started

2. The Martha's Vineyard twenty-miler starts at the Steamship Authority Terminal in Vineyard Haven and traverses the island, ending at Oak Bluffs School, and takes place in mid-February. Information about this opportunity to battle the elements (and prepare for the Boston Marathon) can be found at www.mv20miler.com.
3. The Falmouth Road Race takes place the third Sunday in August. It starts in Woods Hole and finishes seven miles away in Falmouth Heights. Information can be found at https://falmouthroadrace.com.

## Chapter 2. Built in 1890...or Not

4. Witzell, *Walking Tour of Woods Hole*.
5. McAlester, *Field Guide to American Houses*.

## Chapter 3. The Hunt Begins

6. Walker, *Atlas of Barnstable County*, Plate 017.
7. *Falmouth Enterprise*, March 27, 1915.
8. Ibid.
9. *Falmouth Enterprise*, April 25, 1914.

10. The neighboring property, "Parcel B" (#0 Millfield), was purchased in 1913, in the same time frame as "Parcel A" (#22 Millfield). Its owner, F.L. Gifford, applied for a license for a marine railway when Walter applied for a seawall license, offering Gifford access to the water, since his residence on Quissett Avenue was landlocked. Subsequently, Gifford added a boathouse and replaced the marine railway with a dock.

11. Mary Ramsbottom was the first direct link to the Nickersons of Millfield Street. I first interviewed her in 2020, and the answers came slowly. Facts about the family seemed mundane to Mary, so I had to pull on the loose threads of her observations. She hadn't thought about her Woods Hole visit in many years, but her comments provided much-needed context to the story.

12. The Ramsbottom family generously gifted me the teacups, returning them to the house where they once resided. Like the story of the sea captain housing his crew in the attic, the teacups have a murky provenance and will be an interesting research project in the future.

## Chapter 4. Excavating the Facts

13. Records can be found by lot number, name or address, as well as using the location by book and page, and these searches are free to the public at www. barnstabledeeds.org.

14. The newspaper office is located on a now-quiet road that leads up to Highfield House. Sixty years ago, its location across from Falmouth Station put it nearly on top of the train tracks heading into Woods Hole, but now only regional buses stop there. The small headquarters building bustles with activity, especially on Thursdays as the weekly paper prepares for its Friday publication. The *Falmouth Enterprise* has maintained an impressive level of detailed and accurate reporting that is essential to keeping communities engaged and was at the nucleus of fact-finding for this book. The paper's name has evolved over time (*Falmouth Local*, 1886–1895, *Enterprise*, 1895–1927, *Falmouth Enterprise* 1927–present).

15. Information about the newspaper digitization project and the CPFund (Falmouth) can be found at www.cpfundfalmouth.org/falmouth-public-library-digitization-of-historic-documents. Though Massachusetts was an early adopter of localized historic preservation, many other states are now participating.

16. *Falmouth Enterprise*, March 31, 1917.

17. Scanlon, "Portraits of Woods Hole."

18. *Falmouth Enterprise*, June 24, 1916.

19. Ibid., October 14, 1916.

20. Ibid., May 26, 1917.

21. Ibid., September 16, 1916.

22. From Dr Loewl's *Falmouth Enterprise* obituary, August 14, 1947.

23. Ibid., June 9, 1950.

24. Ibid., January 18, 1952.

25. Sanborn Fire Insurance Map, 1923. These maps, published by the Sanborn Map Company, were used by insurance companies to assess financial liabilities of insuring structures in urbanized areas of the United States. They included a rudimentary footprint of buildings and were color-coded to indicate construction materials.
26. McAlester, *Field Guide to American Houses.*
27. *Falmouth Enterprise*, October 19, 1951.

## Chapter 5. Welcome to Woods Hole

28. Schneider, *Enduring Shore.*
29. The *Charles W. Morgan* became a recurring theme in our Woods Hole story. In 2018, shortly after buying the house, we mentioned to friends that we were hoping to buy a Boston Whaler at some point. "Hold it," said Bob, and he scurried off into his house. "I've got a whaler for you!" he proclaimed, presenting us with a large, beautifully framed print of a whaling ship, the *Charles W. Morgan.* "This will be perfect in your new house," he insisted, so we brought it to Massachusetts. It now resides above the carved fireplace mantel in Tom's mother's apartment. At first, the print felt out of place, a bit random. It soon became clear that the *Charles W. Morgan*, its miniature bow adorning the Candle House on Water Street, is part of Woods Hole lore.
30. History.com editors, "Manifest Destiny," www.history.com/topics/19th-century/manifest-destiny.
31. U.S. Census data.
32. No one tells the story of how Woods Hole turned bird poop into gold better than Jennifer Stone Gaines, in her piece from the WHHM journal *Spritsail* 21, no. 2 (2007), a highly recommended read.

## Chapter 6. Scientists and Summer People

33. Woods Hole Historical Museum, Fay Family Collection (1790–1976) overview.
34. NOAA Fisheries, www.fisheries.noaa.gov.
35. Woods Hole Oceanographic Institution, www.whoi.edu/what-we-do.
36. History of the Marine Biological Laboratory, "Women at the MBL," https://history.archives.mbl.edu/browse/exhibits/marine-biological-laboratory/women-mbl.
37. Kenney, "Decoding the Woods Hole July 4th Parade."
38. *Falmouth Enterprise*, August 19, 1899.
39. Woods Hole Golf Club, www.woodsholegolfclub.com.
40. From an interview with Dutch Wessner, head groundskeeper, golf pro and director of golf at WHGC for forty-four years, www.wickedlocal.com.

## Chapter 7. Nobska Lighthouse and Its Keeper

41. Cuttyhunk Historical Society.

42. New England Lighthouses, www.newenglandlighthouses.net.

43. The initial discovery of this fascinating story came from an article written by Brian Melville Nickerson for the Nickerson Family Association newsletter (*Three Nickersons Play Roles in Nobska Point Light*, April 5, 2017). Brian Nickerson was a founding board member of the Friends of Nobska Light, largely responsible for the sympathetic restoration of the complex completed in 2023. Archived newspapers from 1859 filled in the gaps of the murder trial.

44. *Barnstable Patriot*, August 2, 1859, reprinted from the *Yarmouth Register*, and drawing from reporting from *Cape Breton News*.

45. Ibid.

46. Ibid.

47. Ibid.

48. Explanation of the crew's behavior was drawn from assorted articles, but primarily from the *Yarmouth Register*, September 16, 1859, and reprinted four days later in the *Barnstable Patriot*.

49. As reported in the *Yarmouth Register*, September 9, 1859 (*Barnstable Patriot*, September 13, 1859).

50. Ibid.

51. Ibid.

52. Ibid., September 23, 1859.

53. *Falmouth Enterprise*, May 20, 1911.

54. Lighthouse Friends, www.lighthousefriends.com.

55. Ibid.

56. New England Lighthouses, "History of Nobska Point Light, Woods Hole, Massachusetts," www.newenglandlighthouses.net/nobska-point-light-history.

57. Ibid. The original 1908 article has not been located, however.

58. On February 22, 1908, *Falmouth Enterprise* reported that the fog signal was out of order for several days, requiring the bell be rung by hand, no doubt contributing to the Board's concern.

59. From a petition letter to the Lighthouse Board in Washington, published in the *Boston Evening Transcript* on January 28, 1910.

60. *Falmouth Enterprise*, May 20, 1911.

61. Ibid.

62. Lighthouse Friends, www.lighthousefriends.com.

## 8. The Nickersons of Woods Hole

63. Tocqueville quote from *New Yorker* article, "Our Obsession with Ancestry Has Some Twisted Roots," by Maya Jasanoff, May 2, 2022.

64. Letter from Thomas E. Small to Oliver Nickerson on December 13, 1910, from Nickerson files.

65. Specifics about Vesta Nickerson's life primarily come from U.S. Census data and her obituary in the *Falmouth Enterprise*, October 31, 1935.
66. Allen, "Eugenics and American Social History."
67. *Falmouth Enterprise*, June 20, 1896.
68. *Falmouth Enterprise*, September 7, 1906.
69. Ibid.
70. Specifics about Nettie Nickerson's life are drawn from U.S. Census data, the Falmouth Annual Report, *Falmouth Enterprise* and a wide assortment of Washington, D.C. newspapers. Ancestry.com was the main source of resources documenting her evolving marital status.
71. *The Many Lives of George Washington's Townhouses on Capitol Hill* (www.streetsofwashington) with additional details found on the website www.mountvernon.org. During the burning of Washington, D.C., by the British in 1814, valuable documents from the Capitol were hidden in the townhomes, but the British burned them as well, so the documents were lost. In 1834, Admiral Charles Wilke, Antarctic explorer, lived there, which is noted on the plaque commemorating George Washington's buildings, donated by the District of Columbia in 1932.
72. Beer consumption statistics vary by quantity, but mostly show a sharp increase in beer consumption at the turn of the twentieth century, including www.statistica.com and www.api.nsju.org.ua
73. *Washington Post*, July 1, 1908.
74. Ibid., May 8, 1909.
75. Ibid., December 15, 1909.
76. Ibid., November 22, 1912.
77. Ibid.
78. Ibid.
79. Ibid., December 14, 1912.
80. Ibid., March 28, 1913.
81. Ibid., July 29, 1914.
82. The particulars about Nellie and Ruth's difficult circumstances came mostly from U.S. Census data and vital records found on Ancestry.com. Piecing together the end-of-life narrative was a result of multiple cemetery visits and sleuthing through old directories.

## Chapter 9. Walter Nickerson at the Helm

83. Register of Civil, Military, and Naval Service, Contract #4101.
84. From Oscar Hilton interview.
85. *Falmouth Enterprise*, November 18, 1916.
86. From the Nickerson Family Association file on Walter E. Nickerson, in Chatham, Massachusetts.
87. *Falmouth Enterprise*, February 17, 1894.
88. Interview with Prince Crowell, the *Yarmouth Register.*

89. *Falmouth Enterprise*, March 18, 1911.
90. Ibid., August 3, 1901.
91. Ibid., April 28, 1906.
92. Ibid., January 6, 1912.
93. Ibid., September 11, 1897.
94. Ibid., July 11, 1896.
95. Ibid., August 24, 1901.
96. Ibid., July 14, 1906.
97. As John Valois noted in his piece "Woods Hole Yacht Club: Early Years" in *Woods Hole Reflections* (edited by Mary Lou Smith), 128.

## Chapter 10. The Dawn of a New Century

98. *Falmouth Enterprise*, March 11, 1905.
99. Ibid., March 25, 1938.
100. Ibid., December 4, 1909.
101. *Falmouth Annual Report*, December 31, 1909.
102. *Boston Globe*, October 23, 1911.
103. *Falmouth Enterprise*, November 2, 1912.

## Chapter 11. Nugents in the New World

104. Ford, *History of the Town of Clinton*.
105. Ancestry.com.
106. Daly, "Black Cholera Comes to the Central Valley."
107. Ford, *History of the Town of Clinton*.
108. Ibid.
109. Details about the building of the Wachusetts Dam can be found on Paul Marrone's exceptional website www.beforetherewasadam.com. Primary source materials came from the Massachusetts Digital Collection at www.digitalcommonwealth.org.
110. Ibid.
111. Ingano, "Clinton's Catholic Crusader."
112. Ibid.
113. Ibid
114. Ibid.
115. The rectory on Chestnut Street was originally built as the home of Horatio Bigelow, town benefactor. It served as the rectory until November 2023, when it was razed with little fanfare

## Chapter 12. The House Gets Built and Storms Are Brewing

116. St. Patrick's Parish History.
117. Ibid.

118. Specifics about all these transactions can be found on the Barnstable Registry of Deeds by searching the names of the parties involved.

119. *Falmouth Enterprise*, April 1, 1916.

120. Ibid, May 31, 1919.

121. Linda Lehy, whose family lived at 24 Millfield in the 1920s, was quoted in a 1991 article, specifics lost.

122. There is a riveting description of the only enemy attack on U.S. soil during World War I in Ethan Genter's article "A Century Ago, Orleans Was Under Attack," published on July 20, 2019, in the *Cape Cod Times*.

123. *Falmouth Enterprise*, October 20, 1917.

124. *St. Louis Globe-Democrat*, July 28, 1947.

125. *Falmouth Enterprise*, February 21, 1925.

126. Ibid., February 28, 1925.

127. Ibid., February 21, 1925.

128. This information came to light when the newspaper reported on the sisters' attendance at an anniversary dinner, held at the Coonamessett Inn in Falmouth (*Falmouth Enterprise*, February 17, 1956).

129. *Falmouth Enterprise*, September 23, 1938.

130. Ibid.

131. Strong, "Personal Account of the 1938 Hurricane."

132. For an incredible narrative about the effects of the Great Hurricane of 1938 on coastal New England, I highly recommend reading R.A. Scotti's recount in *Sudden Sea: The Great Hurricane of 1938*. It reads like a mystery, though the high toll on life and property is well known upfront. It remains a favorite read, regardless of the terrifying topic, and continues to inspire my writing.

133. Joseph and Frances were married just a few weeks after the 1938 hurricane struck

134. *Falmouth Enterprise*, December 30, 1938.

135. Ibid.

136. Ibid.

137. Ibid., February 24, 1939.

138. Ibid., June 7, 1940.

139. Ibid., September 3, 1954.

140. Ibid.

141. Ibid.

142. Ibid., January 14, 1955.

143. Falmouth Annual Reports, 1933–1940.

144. NOAA Fisheries, "World Wars Impact Woods Hole Fisheries Lab," January 13, 2022, www.fisheries.noaa.gov/feature-story/world-wars-impact-woods-hole-fisheries-lab.

145. *Falmouth Enterprise*, June 22, 1945.

146. Ibid.

### Chapter 13. Bohemians at the Gate

147. Digital Commonwealth, www.digitalcommonwealth.org.
148. *Falmouth Enterprise*, December 5, 1935.
149. Ibid., March 26, 1936.
150. Ibid., May 21, 1936.
151. Ibid.
152. Details about the life of Aaron Nusbaum came from a wide range of sources, including his obituary, Ancestry and his daughter-in-law's memoir.
153. Valois, "Centennial History of the Woods Hole Yacht Club."
154. Ibid., May 13, 1938.
155. *Falmouth Enterprise,* December 17, 1937
156. Ibid., June 24, 1955.
157. Ibid., June 9, 1950.
158. Ibid., December 12, 1952.

### Chapter 14. Modern History: The Lawrences and Roslanskys

159. Details about the Lawrence family comes mostly from "Reflections of a Woods Hole Boy: Childhood Reminiscences of Frederick VanBuren Lawrence (1908–1991)," published in *Spritsail* 10, no. 2 (2008).
160. Ibid., 17.
161. Ibid., 13.
162. Ibid., 22.
163. Ibid., 27.
164. *Falmouth Enterprise*, January 18, 1952.
165. Information about the lives of John and Priscilla Roslansky comes from articles and tributes in the local papers, as well as conversations with their son, Bill Roslansky, who still resides in Woods Hole.
166. Tribute to Priscilla Fenn Roslansky posted at www.chapmanfuneral.com/obituaries.

### Chapter 15. Cape Cod in a Nut (or Clam) Shell

167. Of course, viewing Cape Cod in this way places Woods Hole squarely in the "armpit" of the peninsula, which it assuredly is not!
168. *New Nationalism*, 1910.
169. Colt, *Big House.*

### Chapter 16. Why Woods Hole Matters: The Future Is Now

170. Schneider, *Enduring Shore.*
171. Woods Hole Oceanographic Institution, "Underwater Vehicles," www.whoi.edu/what-we-do/explore/underwater-vehicles.

172. Like all great local legends, there are variations on the story of how, where and when Tommy Leonard crystalized his vision for the Falmouth Road Race. There is consensus, though, on the enormous size of Leonard's heart and his undying commitment to running and to Falmouth. That commitment appears to be contagious, as Frank Shorter himself moved to Falmouth from Boulder, Colorado, in 2021.

173. From Judy Laster's notes.

174. https://capecodexplore.com/woods-hole-film-festival/.

175. Resilient Woods Hole, https://resilientwoodshole.org.

176. Ibid.

## Chapter 17. Why Historic Preservation Matters: Improving Our Future by Preserving Our Past

177. George Washington's Mount Vernon, "The Early History of the Mount Vernon Ladies Association," https://www.mountvernon.org/preservation/mount-vernon-ladies-association/early-history/.

178. National Trust for Historic Preservation, https://savingplaces.org.

179. *Life* magazine interview with Jacqueline Kennedy, September 1, 1962.

180. The White House Historical Association, www.whitehousehistory.org. Full disclosure: for several years, I served as the director of retail operations, where my most important responsibility was to keep our shops in stock with the Official White House Christmas Ornaments from 1981 to present.

181. Letter from Jacqueline Kennedy to Mayor Beame, February 24, 1975.

182. Witzell, *Walking Tour of Woods Hole*.

183. Ibid.

184. Diana Handy Goodhue on *Growing Up in Woods Hole…I Remember* Facebook group.

185. Luey, *House Stories*.

186. https://carlelefante.com

187. Mrs. Kennedy letter to David Finley, April 18, 1962.

188. Preservation Green Lab, "The Greenest Building: Quantifying the Environmental Value of Building Reuse," www.living-future.org/wp-content/uploads/2022/05/The_Greenest_Building.pdf.

189. Ibid.

190. Ibid.

191. National Trust for Historic Preservation, https://savingplaces.org.

# SELECTED BIBLIOGRAPHY

## *Books and Articles*

Allee, M.H. *Jane's Island.* Boston: Houghton Mifflin Company, 1931.

Allen, G.E. "Eugenics and American Social History, 1880–1950." *Genome* 31, no. 2 (1989): 89–156. pubmed.ncbi.nlm.nih.gov/2698847/.

Anonymous. "WWI U-boats off the New England Coast." *Spritsail* 32, no. 1 (2018).

Barbo, T.M. *Hidden History of Cape Cod.* Charleston, SC: The History Press, 2015.

Beran, M.K. *Wasps: The Spendors and Miseries of an American Aristocracy.* New York: Pegasus Books, 2021.

Beston, H. *The Outermost House: A Year of Life on the Great Beach of Cape Cod.* New York: Doubleday and Duran, 1928.

Carnevale, B. *Nobska.* Conneaut Lake, PA: Page Publishing, 2021.

Clark, J. "An Early History of the Woods Hole Yacht Club on Its 125th Anniversary." *Spritsail* 36, no. 2 (2022).

Colt, G.H. *The Big House: A Century of Life of an American Summer Home.* New York: Scribner, 2003.

Daly, Walter J. "Black Cholera Comes to the Central Valley of America." *Transactions of the Americal Clinical and Climatological Association* 119 (2008): 143–153. https://www.ncbi.nlm.nih.gov/pmc/articles/PMC2394684/

DeFerrari, J. "The Many Lives of George Washington's Townhouses on Capitol Hill." *Streets of Washington*, April 10, 2019. www.streetsofwashington.com.

Epstein, D. "Memories of the Woods Hole Yacht Club" *Spritsail* 36, no. 2 (2022).

Falmouth Historical Society. *Legendary Locals of Falmouth.* Charleston, SC: Arcadia Publishing, 2013.

Ford, A.E. *History of the Town of Clinton, Massachusetts 1653–1865.* Clinton, MA: Press of W.J. Coulter, 1896.

Gaines, J.S. "Pacific Guano Factory." *Spritsail* 21, no. 2 (2007).

———. "Whaling." *Spritsail* 21, no. 2 (2007).

Hain, J. "Rachel Carson and Woods Hole." *Spritsail* 27, no. 2 (2013).

Herrera, H. *Upper Bohemia: A Memoir.* New York: Simon & Schuster, 2022.

Ingano, T. "Clinton's Catholic Crusader, Father John O'Keefe." *Worcester Telegram & Gazette,* May 22, 2020.

Jenkins, C. "The Development of Falmouth as a Summer Resort." *Spritsail* 6, no. 1 (1992).

Johnson, A. *A House by the Shore: Twelve Years in the Hebrides.* London: Victor Gollancz, 1986.

Kenney, Diana. "Decoding the Woods Hole July 4th Parade." University of Chicago Marine Biological Lab. June 6, 2016. https://www.mbl.edu/news/decoding-woods-hole-july-4th-parade

Lawrence, F.V. "Reflections of a Woods Hole Boy—Childhood Reminiscences of Frederick VanBuren Lawrence (1908–1991)." *Spritsail* 22, no. 2 (2008).

Lester, J. "Thirty Years of the Woods Hole Film Festival." *Spritsail* 34, no. 2 (2021).

Lewis, A.H. *The Day They Shook the Plum Tree.* San Diego: Harcourt, Brace & World, 1963.

Littel, B. "Early Days of Racing in Woods Hole." *Spritsail* 10, no. 2. 1996.

Luey, B. *House Stories: The Meanings of Home in a New England Town.* Amherst, MA: Bright Leaf Imprint, 2017.

McAlester, V.S. *A Field Guide to American Houses (Revised): The Definitive Guide to Identifying and Understanding America's Domestic Architecture.* New York: Knopf, 2015.

McLaughlin, J.A. "The Angelus Bell Tower and Mary Garden in Woods Hole." *Spritsail* 6, no. 2 (1992).

———. *St. Joseph's Church, Woods Hole, Massachusetts: A History, 1882–1982.* Woods Hole, MA: The Church, 1982.

McPhee, M.R. *When Evil Rules: A True Story of Vengeance and Murder on Cape Cod.* New York: St. Martin's Griffin, 2009.

Nichols, W.J. *Blue Mind: The Surprising Science That Shows How Being Near, In, On, or Under Water Can Make You Happier, Healthier, More Connected, and Better at What You Do.* New York: Little, Brown and Company, 2014.

Norman, D. *Encounters: A Memoir.* Orlando, FL: Harcourt Brace Jovanovich, 1987.

Palladino, E. *Lost Towns of the Swift River Valley: Drowned by the Quabbin.* Charleston, SC: The History Press, 2022.

Potter, E.T. "Hurricane 1938." *Spritsail* 3, no. 1 (1989).

Scanlon, D.G. "Portraits of Woods Hole: The Legacy of Franklin Lewis Gifford." *Spritsail* 25, no. 2 (2011).

Schneider, P. *The Enduring Shore: A History of Cape Cod, Martha's Vineyard, and Nantucket.* New York: Holt Paperbacks, 2001.

Scotti, R. *Sudden Sea: The Great Hurricane of 1938.* New York: Little, Brown and Company, 2003.

Smith, M.L. *Woods Hole Reflections.* Woods Hole, MA: Woods Hole Historical Collection, 1983.

Stetson, J.G. "Woods Hole in World War II." *Spritsail* 25, no. 1 (2011).

Strong, D.O. "Personal Account of the 1938 Hurricane." *Spritsail* 19, no. 1 (2005).

Thoreau, H.D. *Cape Cod.* New York: Heritage Press, 1968. (originally published in 1865)

Valois, J. "The Centennial History of the Woods Hole Yacht Club." *Spritsail* 10, no. 2 (1996).

Walker, G.H. *Atlas of Barnstable County, Massachusetts.* Boston: Walker Lithograph & Publishing Company, 1910.

Ward, M.C. "Falmouth in World War I." *Spritsail* 32, no. 1 (2018).

Wilding, D. *Shipwrecks of Cape Cod: Stories of Tragedy and Triumph.* Charleston, SC: The History Press, 2021.

Williams, J.T. *The Shores of Bohemia: A Cape Cod Story, 1910–1960.* New York: Farrar, Straus and Giroux, 2022.

Witzell, S. *Walking Tour of Woods Hole Village, Including a Brief History.* Woods Hole, MA: Woods Hole Museum Collection, 2013.

## Websites

Ancestry | www.ancestry.com

ASICS Falmouth Road Race | https://falmouthroadrace.com

Cape Cod Xplore | https://capecodxplore.com

Digital Commonwealth | www.digitalcommonwealth.org

Falmouth CPFund | www.cpfundfalmouth.org

Falmouth, MA | www.falmouthma.gov

Falmouth Public Library | www.falmouthpubliclibrary.org

George Washington's Mount Vernon | www.mountvernon.org

Historic New England | www.historicnewengland.org

History | www.history.com

Lighthouse Friends | www.lighthousefriends.com

MV Winter Classic | www.mv20miler.com

National Trust for Historic Preservation | https://savingplaces.org

New England Lighthouses: A Virtual Guide | www.newenglandlighthouses.net

Newspapers | www.newspapers.com

NOAA Fisheries | www.fisheries.noaa.gov

Saint Patrick Parish | www.saintpatrickparish.com

Streets of Washington | www.streetsofwashington.com

United States Lighthouse Society Archives | https://uslhs.org/resources/finding_information/libraries_archives/uslhs-archives

Wachusetts Dam & Reservoir | www.beforetherewasadam.com

White House Historical Association | www.whitehousehistory.org

Woods Hole Golf Club | www.woodsholegolfclub.com

Woods Hole Historical Museum | www.woodsholemuseum.com

Woods Hole Oceanographic Institution | www.whoi.edu

## Publications/Periodicals

*Barnstable Patriot*, founded in 1830, Cape Cod's oldest newspaper

*Boston Evening Transcript*

*Boston Globe*

*Cape Cod Times*

*Evening Star* (defunct daily afternoon newspaper in Washington, D.C.)

*Falmouth Enterprise* (published weekly since 1895)

Sanborn Fire Insurance Maps (Library of Congress)

*Spritsail* (Journal published biannually by the Woods Hole Historical Museum)

*Town of Falmouth Annual Report*

*Washington Post*

*Washington Times*

*Yarmouth Register*

## Museums/Associations/Archives

Arlington Historical Society | Arlington, VA

Barnstable County, Registry of Deeds,

Capitol Hill Restoration Society | Washington, D.C.

Clinton Historical Society | Clinton, MA

Cuttyhunk Historical Society | Cuttyhunk, MA
Friends of Nobska Light | Falmouth, MA
Massachusetts State Archives | Boston, MA
Museums on the Green | Falmouth, MA
National Archives (NARA) | Washington, DC
New York Landmark Preservation Commission | NYC
Nickerson Family Association | Chatham, MA
White House Historical Association | Washington, D.C.
Woods Hole Historical Museum | Woods Hole, MA
Woods Hole Library | Woods Hole, MA

## Churches and Cemeteries

Church of the Messiah | Woods Hole, MA
Fairview Cemetery | Dalton, MA
Lawn Cemetery | Beaver Dam, PA
Lindenwood Cemetery | Stoneham, MA
Mount Auburn Cemetery | Cambridge, MA
Old Stone Church | West Boylston, MA
Pleasant Valley Cemetery | Olean, NY
St. Francis Xavier Cemetery | Centreville, MA
St. John's Cemetery | Lancaster, MA
St. John the Evangelist Church | Clinton, MA
St. Joseph's Church | Woods Hole, MA
Woods Hole Village Cemetery (Church of the Messiah Memorial Garden) | Woods
    Hole, MA

## Interviews

James Grotkowski
William H. Hough
Terrance Ingano
Paul Marrone
Mary Byrne Ramsbottom
Sara Ramsbottom
William Roslansky
Howard C. Young III

# Index

# About the Author

A series of serendipitous happenings led to the purchase of a grand old house in Woods Hole in 2018. Following her career as a retail executive, Elizabeth Sheehy turned to writing full time to tell the story of people she just met, long dead and nearly forgotten. A lifelong writer and a lover of puzzles and mysteries, she put her Trinity College history degree to work to uncover the fascinating lives of the Nickersons and the Nugents from one hundred years ago. Elizabeth grew up in Northern California with English parents who passed down to her their passion for history. She and her husband split their time between Virginia and Massachusetts.